'If you're a business owner or manager, Shivani's ideas will rock your world.'
Dale Beaumont, founder and CEO of Business Blueprint®

'Shivani is an exceptional leader who cares deeply about the transformation of people and the impact they can have in our businesses and communities. When Shivani speaks, we should listen!'
Emma Isaacs, founder and CEO, Business Chicks

'Both practical and transformative and a must read to drive your team towards excellence. It provides you with simple people strategies.'
Verne Harnish, founder of Entrepreneurs' Organization (EO) and Scaling Up. Bestselling author of *Scaling Up* (*Rockefeller Habits 2.0*).

GETTING YOUR
PEOPLE
TO STEP UP

GETTING YOUR
PEOPLE
TO STEP UP

7 Simple Strategies

to **Attract** and **Keep**

Your **Key Talent**

Shivani Gupta

WILEY

First published in 2024 by John Wiley & Sons Australia, Ltd
Level 4, 600 Bourke St, Melbourne, Victoria 3000, Australia

Typeset in Garamond Premier Pro 12/16pt

© John Wiley & Sons Australia, Ltd, 2024

The moral rights of the author have been asserted

ISBN: 978-1-394-24875-9

Cover design by Wiley

Disclaimer

The material in this publication is of the nature of general comment only, and does not represent professional advice. It is not intended to provide specific guidance for particular circumstances and it should not be relied on as the basis for any decision to take action or not take action on any matter which it covers. Readers should obtain professional advice where appropriate, before making any such decision. To the maximum extent permitted by law, the author and publisher disclaim all responsibility and liability to any person, arising directly or indirectly from any person taking or not taking action based on the information in this publication.

CONTENTS

ACKNOWLEDGEMENTS

To my amazing husband Scott, for always encouraging and believing in me.

To my wonderful children, Shanti and Om — you light up my life.

To my mum and dad, for the values you instilled in me.

To my clients — your trust in my expertise and your feedback has helped me grow and evolve.

To the thought leaders whose insights have deepened my knowledge.

To my friends — your guidance and love is appreciated.

To the people who have worked with me and for me both in the past and present: This book is one of the outcomes of our conversations and shared experiences. I have learned so much about people because of you, even the hard lessons.

To the team at Wiley, my publisher, especially Lucy and Leigh — your support with this book has been invaluable.

This book would not have come to life without you, the reader — the business leader and owner. Thank you in advance for picking it up. I hope you find a key takeaway you can use to grow your business and your people.

INTRODUCTION

People, people, people.

Attracting and retaining great people is becoming more difficult. This has become both a challenge and a risk for the growth of businesses. According to the 2024 edition of the KPMG report 'Keeping us up at night', one of the top issues right now for most businesses in Australia is how to find the right people, retain them and get them to perform the right tasks well.

People discovered during the pandemic that they have more career options than they might have thought. Working from home and virtual working models became the norm, and the demand for skilled people began to outstrip supply. There is a high degree of burnout in many industries as people's resilience has eroded away. And throughout and following the pandemic, the world has witnessed a 'Great Resignation' period, where millions of people started to quit their jobs.

As a result, attracting and retaining great people has become stressful and expensive for many businesses. The cost of bringing a new hire from the hiring stage through to delivering a high-performance output can be up to five times their salary, depending on your industry. This is extremely high and for many businesses can make or break your business.

Your people can be either assets or liabilities

At some point in your life, you made a decision to step into being a business leader or owner.

You may have yearned for more freedom, more influence, better systems, better marketing, better leadership and better management of what should be your biggest asset — your people.

Many businesses believe that people are their number one asset. You might also share that belief. In my experience, however, people can be either your biggest asset or your biggest liability.

You may have some people without whom you cannot run your business or manage your people. Some people jump on problems straight away and, in some instances, they may even be able to predict that a problem is arising. They are eager to fix the issue as quickly as possible so that your business can run faster and better. These people are your assets.

And there are others who you may wish just weren't there as they cause you more work than they produce. These people may have the skills to solve a problem, but they may be reluctant to fix the problem. They want to blame others for why the problem exists in the first place, blame the system, or even blame you as the business leader or owner. These people are your liabilities.

When people do the right things, are motivated to work hard and are passionate about the work they do, these people are your assets. They are the people that you love working with. They are the ones that you hope will stay in your business forever. But when the challenging, noisy people that are liabilities are in full force, it can cause you stress and maybe even sleepless nights. I know. I have had them!

You may ask yourself, 'Surely this is not the same person that I interviewed only a few months ago?' And then you start to develop headaches when dealing with them and wonder how to manage them out of your business and your life.

This book is designed for business leaders and owners of small to medium-sized businesses who want to have more people that are assets and less people that are liabilities.

Growing your business through early challenges

As your business starts to grow, there are all sorts of problems to solve. These issues may arise daily. You may find that you are working harder than ever before while trying to motivate the people in the business. Some of these people take up your energy and consume more time in your diary than they give.

And sometimes, when are you are hiring people and trying to attract them into your business, you feel desperate, especially if you don't have many options due to the candidates that have applied. You are happy to hire anyone, as long as they have a pulse!

As your business grows, people management is a typical growth pain point for business leaders and business owners, but without overcoming this challenge you cannot scale to the next level of growth.

I have found myself in this position many times over the last 20 years. At times, I have not been able to find the right person or, when I did, they left because my retention strategy did not work (or, to be honest, I didn't have one at the time).

Sometimes you may wonder if you made the right choice stepping into the role of being a business leader or owning a business. Then the thought of having lots of bosses crosses your mind and you reconnect to why you took this path in the first place. So, you put these thoughts aside and then refocus and, once again, you are 'head down' solving these people problems so your business can grow.

To grow successfully, you need the right people in the right jobs doing the right things at the right time to ensure that your business needs are being met.

Consider this example. You find yourself pacing your lounge room and kitchen. You look at the clock and it is 3am. You've been up for at least two hours already. You are feeling stressed and don't know how to slow down your mind, which is racing through all sorts of scenarios because you think you are about to lose John and Amanda from your business. This repeated thought alone gets your heart rate up.

They are both key leaders and have grown with you and the business. They are dedicated, highly engaged and productive. Well, at least that is what you thought.

John came into your office four days ago and announced to you sheepishly that he has been offered a better job with more money. He says he is thinking of taking it because he has been with you for five years now and perhaps it is time for a change. You are disappointed, although you are trying not to alienate him with your disappointment as you absorb the news. You thought John was going to be there forever and had plans for him taking on more. And he had not indicated that he was unhappy at any stage, or that he was thinking of leaving.

Amanda, on the other hand, has not been fully present at work for a few weeks now. She has been doing all the tasks but her normal high levels of energy have been missing. She says it has nothing to do with work and that her home is stressful at present. You know her partner works in a high-paying job and earns more than her, and they are also raising two young children while managing their careers.

You have asked her several times if she needs anything, and she always says she will let you know if she does. She says her husband has suggested she could cut down her days at work to make more time for raising their family, but she is not sure she wants to do that. You have thought about letting her work four days a week instead of five if she requests it. What if she wants to quit? She runs most of the operations and is your right-hand person.

And what if they both leave within the next two weeks, which is the notice they have to give? You find yourself thinking your contract is not right. You need a year's notice to replace people like John and Amanda, which seems impossible anyway.

The business you have worked so hard to build is based on the foundation of people like John and Amanda. If they both left, it would take you months or maybe years to get other people trained to the same skill level and with the same attitude.

You find yourself wondering, 'Is there something I'm missing?' 'Have I missed the signs?' 'Did I forget to love my best people?' 'Why did I not create a succession plan?'

You realise that in the last few months, you have regained your family and work balance, but if John and Amanda leave you may go back to doing the things you thought you had finally delegated. Your partner and kids see more of you now, but what if that changes as a result of this sudden shift in your business?

Your head is still spinning. You have a big day tomorrow, with key meetings, although you aren't sure how to get yourself back to sleep…

Can you relate to any of these thoughts? I have found myself in this situation many times, and this is the reason I wanted to write this book.

Not every idea I share will work for your people or your business — and some you may have already implemented. So, I am going to offer you a variety of ideas, actions and models to try, which you can review so you can decide which ones you want to implement.

How to use this book

In this book, I want to share with you 7 simple strategies that may help you attract and retain great people, and to develop people that can step up.

Each chapter has a number of suggested actions you may want to implement to improve the people you hire and retain. As you are reading through the suggested actions, I suggest that you focus on one action per chapter at first. If you are experiencing overwhelm, then just pick one action to implement from the book and see where that takes you. My goal for any book I read is that I get a minimum of one good idea that I can use in my business, family or personal life, and I apply it straight away. That is my intention for you as the reader of this book.

This book is practical. I share what I have done when it comes to attracting and retaining people, and getting people to step up. I will be honest about what has worked for me and what has not; what I did that worked and where I failed (sometimes miserably!). I am going to be vulnerable, thanks to Brené Brown — who I love and appreciate for teaching me about the importance of vulnerability.

I highlight examples from some of the world's biggest companies that you can aspire to emulate and learn from. I share examples from other small business leaders and owners, some of whom I have had the opportunity to work with, as well as exploring what well-known leaders and businesses are implementing to attract the right people, retain these people and get them to step up. I also share some of the models, theories and parables I have found useful so you can gain further insight into how to get people to step up.

At the end of each chapter, I provide several coaching questions I would be asking if you and I were sitting in a 1:1 coaching session. You might find it most helpful to answer these in a journal so you can identify gaps that you can action.

In this book, we will spend time breaking down some myths and creating new strategies around finding and keeping the best people, and bridging the gap between your desired results and the actual results you can achieve if you have high-performing people.

I also want to acknowledge YOU at this point. You are reading this book as part of wanting to continue to grow and learn, and try things in a different way when it comes to the people in your business. Give yourself a pat on the back for wanting to keep learning and trying new things.

Together, we can unlock the potential of your most valuable asset — some of your amazing people.

Vamos! Allons-y! Andiamo! Chalo! Let's go!

PART I

ATTRACTING THE RIGHT PEOPLE

CHAPTER 1

PEOPLE NEED SOMETHING TO BELIEVE IN

Creating a shared vision

I love working with businesses. I love the journey of walking into a business that isn't performing very well, finding the gaps in the way they operate and finding ways to close those gaps. These gaps are where the opportunities lie. Each time, I ask myself, 'How can I fix this business, help its people in the process and make it more profitable?'

I have taken several businesses that were underperforming and, through the work I do with my clients, fixed them up so they generate more profit.

I call this process 'creating a shared vision'.

In order for a shared vision to work, we need two things:

1.   We need to be clear what the vision is.

2.   We need our people to be able to see it so they can help us reach that vision.

Our people need a vision to believe in. Why? Because people want and need something to believe in.

As a personal example, I like to renovate properties — and to be successful when renovating, I try and create a clear vision of the outcome. I also need the contractors I hire (my people) to see what I am seeing. I do this by creating a Pinterest board with images of the end product I envision after the renovation, and I share this Pinterest board with the contractors for each project.

A property that is rundown and needs work aesthetically is my ideal property. The three changes I usually make are adding a new kitchen, painting inside and out, and redoing the floors or windows as these improvements add the most value to a property. Once the contractors have seen my vision — which is what I see — the work starts to be in 'flow' as we are all working towards the same vision. When I have not been able to get a clear vision when viewing a property or a business, I have made the decision to not buy that property.

The same applies in business. For example, I looked at purchasing a recruitment business that looked great on the outset but after conducting my due diligence process, there was not much value in the business besides the business owner and her reputation. I thought that it was overpriced at $1 million, mainly because I could not see the vision of the current owner, nor could I see the gaps that I could fix. And if I can't see the vision, how do I show the people who are working within that business what to see? Simple answer, I can't. And if they can't see it, they won't believe in it — and the business will not work or grow.

I have also got the vision exercise wrong before. I once bought a kids' playcentre without having clarity on my vision. I got so excited about finding the operational gaps I could fix that I was blindsided by the lack of vision.

After I bought the business, I realised it needed a large cash injection, which I had not catered for as I was trying to balance too many other responsibilities at the same time. These responsibilities included raising two small children, running two other growing businesses and fully renovating our home, for which I was the project manager. As I had no vision, I found it difficult to get the people in the business to see the vision and be inspired. And over the course of almost a year, when I was running that business without a vision, it was difficult to inspire the people within the business as they didn't know what they were working towards.

In hindsight, the vision was a simple one and should have been clear to me: It was to make kids (and their parents) happy. However, I was so focused on small profit-making initiatives that did not lead anywhere (such as providing the right coffee and food for the parents) that I failed to engage the people working within the business. Instead of getting excited about working there each day, my people were disengaged and could not see what I was trying to create — which is no surprise, as I was also disengaged with my vision.

Operational fixes are not that inspiring (though identifying them can feel amazing). This playcentre failure cost me a lot of money and made a dent in my confidence — and to be brutally honest, the failure dented my ego as well. I hired a great coach to help me deal with this failure, who advised me to learn from the experience so I didn't repeat the same mistake. I indeed learned a valuable and expensive lesson: Don't start a business if you have no vision. (I also learned about the importance of detailed due diligence to get an understanding of the need for future cash injections!)

As a business leader and owner, you need to see the vision for your business and be able to get your people to see it too.

Setting your vision

I get asked by many people if a great manager can set the vision. I believe the difference between a leader (or business owner) and a manager (who the leader or business owner hires to implement the vision) is that a leader sets the direction (of the vision) and the manager sets the speed at which you will travel to achieve your vision.

The direction sets a clear path for you to take to achieve the vision. Leaders are responsible for defining the vision, mission and long-term goals of the business, guiding its strategic direction, and inspiring others to follow a shared purpose. They establish the framework within which the business operates, providing clarity of purpose and a sense of direction to align the efforts of its people towards common goals.

Managers, on the other hand, concentrate on the operational aspects of achieving these goals, ensuring allocation of resources, coordinating tasks, and driving productivity to accomplish the goals set out within specified time frames. While leaders chart the course, managers oversee the pace of progress.

As the business leader and owner, you want to take your business from A to B — this is your vision for the business. For an illustrative example, imagine that you, as a leader (who is responsible for setting the vision), decide to move from Adelaide to Brisbane (both cities in Australia I happen to have lived in — and literally from A to B!). This decision sets the direction of the business.

Once you have set the vision, your manager is responsible for working out how you will move from Adelaide to Brisbane and how you can get there as efficiently and effectively as possible. Are you going to fly? Are you going to drive? Where are you going to stop? How are you going to pay for that? What budget do you need? Who else is coming? They will be considering all the details to realise the vision.

The manager and the people in your business need to see the vision to help you realise your vision. They need to believe in where you're going (which is Brisbane, in this example). As the business leader and owner, you need to help your manager(s) and people to visualise Brisbane and the amazing place it will be.

I frequently use the example of going from A to B and referring to the two as Adelaide to Brisbane in my speaking and coaching work. And as I was writing this chapter, I had an epiphany.

Both my husband and I felt that we wanted to move our family to Brisbane as it had better opportunities for a family of four in terms of work, education and opportunities. We had our Vedic charts done to see which city was best to live in (that is a story for another time!).

We wanted to convince our kids, so we painted a picture of the benefits of living in Brisbane and asked for their input — and they got the visualisation, which we went through with them several times. I even made a PowerPoint presentation (yes, I know that sounds crazy but I wanted to use my speaking abilities to present our vision to them, and not force them to see it). We wanted them to be inspired to move with us and share the vision for the move, not just move because we made them.

One of our kids wanted a house with a pool, and the other wanted a second cat. We ticked these requests off the list for both of them and then we moved. We got our people to see the vision!

When different people see the same vision in different ways

Imagine two people are working on a construction site where a grand temple is being built in hot and dusty conditions.

(continued)

People often stop to ask the workers about what they are doing.

One day, a traveller asks the construction workers, 'What are you building?'

The first construction worker says, 'I'm chipping away at this rock, as you can see. It's hot, dusty and backbreaking work. But I need the money to put food on the table for my family.'

The traveller then asks the second construction worker what they are building.

The second person says, 'I am building a temple where people can come and connect and pray.' They believe in something bigger than a rock. They believe they are building a temple. They believe in a vision.

If you align the names of the key people in your business against the first construction worker and the second construction worker in this parable, how many of each type of person do you have in your business? As leaders and owners, we all want more people with the attitudes of the second construction worker in our business.

Gaudí's visionary legacy

One of my favourite cities in the world is Barcelona, Spain. And one person whose name you cannot escape in Barcelona is the architect Antoni Gaudí.

Gaudí's most famous building, the Sagrada Família, is an example of a vision of artistic brilliance. Located in the heart of Barcelona, this iconic architectural masterpiece is more than just a church. When I stand in front of it, which I have done many times, its beauty always leaves me in awe, despite the thousands of tourists from all over the world who are walking all around me.

When Gaudí took over the project of designing the church in 1883, he transformed it into a visionary work of art. He saw the basilica not just as a place of worship but as a space for creation.

Gaudí's vision for the Sagrada Família extended far beyond his own lifetime. He knew that completing such an ambitious project would take decades, if not centuries. Gaudí saw himself as a part of a larger vision and he believed that the basilica's construction should continue long after his death.

He left behind detailed plans and models, ensuring that future architects and builders could carry on his vision. This type of vision goes beyond the self and links into purpose. In my view, Gaudí's purpose was to help others see what he saw — to finish building what he had started to build.

The Sagrada Família's ongoing construction shares many parallels with business. Business leaders and owners often embark on ambitious projects that require a clear vision to succeed. In much the same way, the basilica's continued construction relies on a network of passionate believers and patrons.

Business leaders and owners are expected to inspire their people to work towards a common vision. To achieve this, they must instil that vision in their people.

In August 2023, I was on a business retreat in Western Australia. I met the CEO of a famous winery, which was a third-generation family business. When speaking to the CEO about finding the right wines for the consumers of the future, he showed me some vines they had recently planted and explained that the resulting wines won't be released in his lifetime.

He said that the business has to think long term and that there was no place for the ego when making these decisions. I found this so inspiring — I could see the legacy he was trying to create. Legacy for me is the impact you have on people long after you are gone. This CEO gave his people a vision to believe in that went beyond himself.

Just as Gaudí aimed to leave a lasting legacy through the basilica, business leaders and owners often work to build something that will endure beyond their lifetimes. When your people see what you are trying to achieve, the hope is that they will feel inspired to share the vision and work towards that shared vision. This shared vision can be incredibly motivating for the people in your business.

Businesses with a clear vision

In today's world, businesses are propelled by their visionary statements, which capture their aspirations and guiding principles. Here are just a few recognisable examples:

- **The Walt Disney Company: 'entertain, inform, and inspire'.**
  Disney's commitment to entertaining, informing and inspiring people worldwide underscores its enduring influence in the realms of theme parks, movies and merchandise.

- **Tesla: 'accelerate the world's transition to sustainable energy'.**
  Tesla's relentless pursuit to accelerate the world's transition to sustainable energy has spurred ground-breaking innovations in electric vehicles and renewable energy solutions.

- **Amazon: 'to be Earth's most customer-centric company'.**
  Amazon's unwavering dedication to being Earth's most customer-centric business has fuelled its reputation for unparalleled customer service and continuous innovation.

- **SpaceX: to build vehicles 'capable of carrying humans to Mars and other destinations in the solar system'.** SpaceX's audacious goal of enabling human travel to Mars and beyond has revolutionised the aerospace industry.

These visionary statements not only define the essence of these businesses but also show their strategic direction as a result.

Small to medium-sized businesses with a clear vision

The following real-life and lived experiences come from some of the people I've had the privilege to work with and who have been willing to share their experiences of developing their business's vision. As business leaders and owners, they have divulged the nuances of their strategic approach towards creating a flourishing business.

- **Kate Save, Be Fit Food:** 'We have an annual strategy session to reinstate our vision with all of our people.'

- **Wes Blundy, Curvy:** 'We communicate our vision through quarterly state of the business meetings.'

- **Scott Orpin, MEGT:** 'To get people to live the vision, we get to know them, coach them and give them room to succeed.'

- **Fiona Anchal, Wholesome Bellies:** 'We have quarterly dinners so we can get together as a group and discuss the vision.'

- **Annika Launay, PDPR Marketing + Creative:** 'We have open two-way communications and live and breathe our vision.'

- **Kate Winter, Champion Web:** 'We have a screening process on how people we hire and their vision aligns with ours.'

- **Liberte Guthrie, Liberte Property & Crossroad Developments:** 'I have a rule and it's that we work with people you like and who get your vision.'

- **Angus Nicol, Black Market Coffee:** 'We walk the talk, which is part of our vision.'

- **Ali Koschel, Hunter New England and Central Coast Primary Health Network (HNECC PHN):** 'Review this context (and make sure the work they do matches our strategy).'

- **Tina Tower, Her Empire Builder:** 'Meet together every 90 days. Have a channel of communication for celebration and connection.'

- **Sam Mathers, Fitter Futures:** 'Hire right. You have an "awesome humans" (no "wankers") policy.'

- **Jane Save, The Save Group:** 'Hire to core values, train on mission, vision and values and lead by example.'

- **Nicole Bryant, The Macro Group:** 'We give examples of values and vision at every meeting. We have a monthly values award.'

Actions

To give your people something to believe in, you need to have a clear vision for your business that you can transform into a shared vision. The two actions I share here are simple yet powerful. They focus on emotional connection, leadership influence and people ownership, which are important in getting your people to see and live the vision once you have developed your vision statement.

#1. Create a clear vision statement

A compelling vision often involves bold and ambitious statements. It needs to inspire and challenge your people to strive for excellence. Developing a clear vision for your business is a crucial step if you want to grow your business and inspire your people.

If you already have a clear vision, this action may help you go deeper into that vision.

Start by reflecting on your personal values, passions and beliefs. For example, try some of these techniques to explore your values:

1. **Self-reflection:** Allocate some time to reflect on your values, passions and beliefs. Consider journalling or engaging in mindfulness practices to delve into your thoughts and feelings. Reflect on past experiences, identifying moments when you felt most aligned with your values and passions. Ask yourself questions such as, 'What activities bring me the most joy?' or 'What principles are important to me?' This process can help you gain clarity on what truly matters to you.

2. **Experiential learning:** Actively engage in new experiences and activities to explore your values, passions and beliefs in action. Volunteer for causes that resonate with you, participate in workshops aligned with your interests, or simply try out different hobbies. Pay attention to how these experiences make you feel and whether they resonate with your core values and passions. Embrace opportunities for growth and self-discovery by stepping outside your comfort zone and embracing new challenges.

3. **Seek feedback and perspective:** Engage in open and honest conversations with your friends, family members, mentors or work colleagues to gain insight into your values, passions and beliefs. Seek feedback on how others perceive your strengths,

interests and values. Their perspectives can offer valuable insights and help you gain a deeper understanding of yourself.

Your vision must align with your core values, as it will be a reflection of you in the business.

Think about why your business exists. What problem does it solve and what needs does it meet? Your vision must be rooted in the purpose of your business.

Where do you want your business to be in the long term? Think about your aspirations, such as where you want to see your market position, revenue, customer impact or industry influence. These goals will help shape your vision.

Think about what makes your business unique. Your vision needs to highlight what qualities set you apart from your competitors.

Consider how your vision will benefit people (both people that work for you and your customers) and the value it will bring to their lives.

Study the vision statements of successful businesses that you admire (you may find my earlier examples a useful place to start as I talk about businesses with a clear vision, such as Disney).

When you have considered these areas, you can start to develop your vision statement. Your vision statement needs to be simple to remember. It has to explain your vision in just one or two sentences.

Your vision statement needs to be forward-looking, outlining what you aim to achieve in the years ahead. It needs to excite and inspire people about what's possible in the future.

Above all, ensure that your vision aligns with the core values and principles of your business as it will serve as a guiding light for your business's actions and decisions.

As a business leader and owner, involve the key people in your business in developing or revising your vision. By engaging with the perspective and inputs from your people, they can contribute to a more detailed and inclusive vision and feel a part of the process. Don't be afraid to dream big and ask for input. Make this your team's vision, not just yours.

Even if you are a leader within an existing business rather than a business owner, you can still follow the same process and ask yourself the same questions to ensure that you understand the business's vision statement, and that you can feel and live the vision of the business.

And if you have influence in the strategic planning process, where the vision is reviewed, take your questions and comments into that discussion. Make sure at the end of that process you believe the vision and you can see other people in the business doing the same.

When I start or take over a business, I sit with a large whiteboard and reflect on all the areas covered in this action so far. This helps me get clarity on who I am, what I want to create (my vision) and how I want to run the business (the business's operations).

One of the businesses I ran was a wellness business where I revised the vision for my people to be inspired — and this revised vision had a 'part of me' in it. The vision I came up with was 'We help people improve their wellness'. That was it. Nothing more. It was beyond any service or product. I wanted to help the people engaging with the business to become more aware of their wellbeing and the strategies they needed to put into place to become healthier inside and out.

#2. Get your people to see the vision

Once you have a clear vision, you need your people to be able to see the vision. You want your people to see what you see. The more people can see your vision, they more they will know what to do in their role in order to help the business achieve that vision. People need something to believe in!

Once you've developed your vision statement, communicate it widely and reiterate it to your people. Encourage discussions, feedback and questions to ensure everyone understands and embraces the vision. You want your people to see the vision and live and breathe it. That is how a vision comes to life.

The best ways to bring your vision to life are storytelling, leading by example and having people take ownership of the vision. This allows your people to see and live the vision.

Storytelling

Sharing stories that demonstrate your vision can help your people see the power of your vision. For example, you might tell a story about why you started the business or use a story to illustrate a transformational moment in your life or the life of another leader — and maybe you can share how that story inspired you to create your business's vision or helps you to live that vision, which makes the vision relatable and memorable. Using examples and the names of people who live the vision and have made a positive impact on the business may enhance this relatability further.

Regularly incorporate these stories into meetings with your people and your communications to keep the vision alive in your people's minds. Repetition of stories is important.

I share stories of my childhood with my people — stories of me being the first woman in my lineage to work, and how honoured I feel and how much I love my work as a result. Work is never a chore for me; it is in fact the opposite. It's a privilege. Understanding what motivates me and why I am so passionate about my work helps my people understand my vision and why I created that vision.

Leading by example

Another way to bring your vision to life is to lead by example. Your actions and behaviours speak louder than words. Your people will look to you as a role model and your example will influence their behaviour and attitudes. This authenticity also includes the times when you fail and are not living the vision. Own it and talk about this failure with your people. They then have an opportunity to see you as an authentic business leader and owner, and you and your vision become more relatable.

I remember being in a team meeting with my key leaders and managers for my wellness business, and I shared that I was not looking after my own wellness despite owning a wellness business. I explained that I felt like a hypocrite regarding the business's vision. I knew I was meant to live the vision, and yet I wasn't.

The people in my team resonated with that honesty and they too shared that many of them felt the same. This strengthened our team bond. We realised that we needed to create more self-care and wellness for ourselves while serving other people's wellness, and so we developed clear actions as a result of that disclosure.

We ended up creating a regular check-in for people in pairs who met weekly for the next few months, which had great results for us individually as well as a management team. This allowed us to reconnect to the vision and start to live it again.

Encouraging people to take ownership of the vision

Another way to get your people to take ownership of their roles and live the vision is by encouraging your people to set personal goals aligned with the vision, which creates a sense of individual and business purpose.

Each quarter, I would ask my managers to share how they are progressing with their personal goals (set at the beginning of each year). I would then share my progress towards my goals for the year, including how, as a business leader and owner, I could help people meet their personal goals. I also encouraged people to help each other in a way that is in alignment with the business's vision.

Case study: Burt's Bees

Cameron Herold's book *Vivid Vision* (2018) is a great resource that outlines a framework for creating a compelling and clear vision for your business and getting your people to see that vision. The company Burt's Bees reminds me of this concept of 'vivid vision'.

Burt's Bees was founded in 1984 by Burt Shavitz and Roxanne Quimby. The business began as a small candle-making business, but it expanded into natural personal care products, such as lip balms, lotions and skincare items. The business's vision was not only about creating natural and sustainable products but also about promoting environmental sustainability.

They implemented what I consider to be the principles of 'vivid vision' in their business:

- **They had clarity of vision:** They were creating natural products but also creating them sustainably. This vision was outlined and communicated to the people consistently.

- **They operated in alignment with their values:** The business was closely aligned with the personal values of both co-founders, who were passionate about environmental sustainability and social responsibility.

- **They utilised storytelling:** Quimby was known as a great storyteller. She often spoke about her experiences and the business's journey, speaking about the importance of natural products and sustainable practices. Her stories made the vision personal and relatable to her people.

- **They involved their people:** All their people got involved in shaping the vision of the business. Quimby encouraged her people to participate in initiatives that aligned with the vision.

- **They led by example:** Quimby actively promoted environmental sustainability and social responsibility by supporting various causes, which further reinforced the business's vision.

I believe that a part of the success of Burt's Bees is due to their vision for the business and the work they did to get their people to see the vision. The business became a well-known brand in the natural personal care industry.

Case study: Warby Parker

In my view, Warby Parker also seems to have applied the concept of 'vivid vision' to revolutionise the eyewear industry by offering high-quality, stylish glasses at affordable prices while integrating a socially conscious business model.

Founded in 2010, the company's vision stemmed from the founders' frustration with the high costs and lack of innovation in the eyewear market. They recognised the opportunity to disrupt the industry by cutting out unnecessary middlemen and offering direct-to-consumer sales.

Key strategies included designing fashionable glasses in-house to reduce costs, implementing a unique 'try at home' program to address online purchasing concerns, and initiating a 'Buy a Pair, Give a Pair' program to donate glasses to those in need. These initiatives not only aligned with their vision but also resonated with customers, leading to rapid growth and the attainment of 'unicorn' status by 2015.

Warby Parker's success underscores the power of a vivid vision to me in driving innovation and creating positive change in traditional industries.

Reflections

As we embark on a coaching journey together, I suggest you create the perfect setting for reflection and growth. We will revisit coaching reflections in each chapter of this book, so you may find you want to come back to this setting again and again.

Remember the importance of your environment, where your thoughts can flow. Find a serene spot, one that resonates with calmness and clarity. It might be a corner of your home, a favourite coffee shop or a bench in a sun-dappled park — anyplace where you can reflect without distractions.

Before diving into the questions that follow, ensure you have a journal and a pen within reach to capture your thoughts. There's something almost magical about the act of writing. It allows your mind to wander through the corridors of possibility.

Now, consider me as your coach. Together, we'll explore questions that will challenge you to dig deeper and view things through a lens of curiosity. This is your moment to be fearless in your inquiry, to confront the realities of your situation, and to uncover the potential.

Ready? Take a deep breath. Centre yourself. With each question, allow your initial response to surface and then go deeper. Ask yourself: Why do I feel this way? What do these thoughts reveal about my current path and the direction I wish to take? How can I align my actions with my core values and vision for success? You may also like to ask the people in the business to reflect on the same questions.

Remember, the insights you gather here are stepping stones towards YOU.

The questions are broken down into several sections. Separating the questions into distinct areas allows for a more structured and focused approach to addressing each aspect of business renovation and vision clarification. By breaking down the discussion into specific topics, we can go deeper into each area, explore relevant questions, and develop actionable insights and strategies. This approach facilitates a more detailed way of looking at important aspects. Additionally, breaking down the discussion into separate sections helps maintain clarity and coherence, making it easier for you to track progress and identify areas for further exploration or improvement.

Prioritising business renovation:

- What are the three significant tasks that you need to focus on right now to renovate your business?

- What are the steps and actions you need to take next?

Clarifying your vision:

- As business owners and leaders, it's essential to have a clear vision for your business. Are you confident in your understanding of your vision? If not, what aspects could use more clarity?

- How can storytelling enhance communication and alignment?

Ensuring alignment with your people:

- Do your people see and understand the vision as you do? If not, what steps can you take to ensure better alignment?

Learning from examples:

- Which examples in this chapter resonate with you the most and compel you to take action?

- How can you draw inspiration from successful stories to guide your strategic decisions?

Reinforcing the vision:

- How much time are you currently dedicating each week to reiterating your vision?

- What can you do to consistently reinforce your vision regularly?

Personal connection to the vision:

- Explore your thoughts and feelings about your vision. What does it mean to you, and how does it align with your ideal future?

Values and guiding principles:

- Identify the values and principles that are most important to you. How do these guide your vision for the business?

Leveraging strengths:

- Reflect on your strengths. Consider what your people may think your strengths are. What might they say?

- How can your unique abilities contribute to realising both your vision and theirs?

Setting aligned goals:

- What goals do you believe align with your shared vision?

- What are the measurable and achievable milestones that contribute to meeting your vision?

Legacy and motivation:

- Consider the legacy you want to leave behind. What is it?

- What motivates and inspires you to work towards
  your vision?

Identifying necessary resources:

- What resources, skills or knowledge do you think you need to
  bring your vision to life?

- What are the necessary tools and capabilities you need
  to succeed?

Anticipating challenges:

- Identify potential obstacles or challenges in achieving your vision.
  How can you proactively address and overcome these hurdles?

Building a support system:

- What kind of support system or network do you need to stay
  committed to your vision?

- What can you do to build a strong support network?

Summary

Having a clear vision is essential, whether you are a business owner or a business leader. A clear, compelling and vivid vision plays a crucial role in steering a business towards success.

Business improvement is a process of small actions that lead to bigger results. Just as a rundown property requires a clear vision for renovation, a business needs a vision to guide its major wins and results. This vision is not only about fixing operational gaps but also about inspiring people and making your business more profitable.

To have a clear vision you and your team can get behind:

- You must be crystal clear about the vision, understanding the underlying details so you can communicate these to your team, which entails more than just a surface-level understanding. It's not enough to have a 'lofty' vision — you need one that is more specific. This involves understanding the principles, values and objectives that shape the vision. Clarity about the vision empowers people and businesses to make decisions, set aligned goals and navigate challenges with confidence.

- Your vision must be communicated effectively to the people in your team, making it visible and inspiring for every person. People need something to believe in, which will instil their belief and commitment in what they are working towards.

Disney, Tesla, Amazon, SpaceX and others have become iconic not just for their products but for the visions they champion. The examples of Burt's Bees and Warby Parker provide insights into how aligning the vision with values, involving people and getting them to see what they stand for, and storytelling and leading by example contribute to a compelling vision.

The vision shared from other small to medium-sized business owners as well as well-known global examples show that these businesses and their leaders and owners don't always get the vision right the first time. Sometimes you need to come up with the vision and then continue to refine it, just like Kate Save at Be Fit Food, who has an 'annual strategy session' that involves refining the shared vision.

A vision is a living thing. Keep sharing it with your people. Keep engaging them in conversations about your vision. Keep talking about it, and get your people to keep talking about it. You cannot have enough conversations about your vision and how to keep working towards that each day. Don't get sick of talking about it. Ever.

CHAPTER 2

THE RIGHT PEOPLE IN THE RIGHT JOBS

Recruiting and incentivising passionate people

How many of you have hired people that you thought were right or even 'perfect' for the job and then, within the space of a few weeks or months, realised you had hired the wrong person? They might be the right person for another job. But you now know that they are definitely not the right person for the job they are in. You might wonder, 'How could this happen when I followed a rigorous recruitment process?'

As a business leader or owner, you are responsible for ensuring you hire the right people — even if you're not doing the hiring yourself. If someone in your team is doing the hiring, you are still responsible for ensuring that people follow the systems and processes so they make the right choice.

As petty as it sounds, sometimes my first reaction is to blame the people I have hired when I realise they are wrong for the job. I find myself asking unhelpful questions, such as, 'Did you manipulate the answers in the interview so you said what I wanted to hear?' It feels like a relationship that had so much potential at the beginning and yet is now doomed, so you might also find yourself thinking, 'You were fine while we were dating—it's only now that I have moved in with you (in other words, moved past the probation period!) that I can see the real you.'

At the end of the day, as a business leader and owner, I am to blame when I hire the wrong person. The 'buck' stops with me. And the buck stops with you as a business leader. And even if a manager did the hiring, the buck still stops with you as you need to implement better systems and training to ensure that your managers hire the right people.

If you're reading this and nodding your head, I get it. I have hired the wrong person so many times. I can be a slow learner, so it took me a while to work out the reasons why this was happening and to learn the lessons from these experiences! The saying (often attributed to Albert Einstein) that 'Insanity is doing the same thing over and over again and expecting different results' seems true in this situation. And insane is how I have felt when I have repeated this mistake.

It is not only an expensive (or extremely expensive) mistake to make; it can also be infuriating and soul destroying, as you may find yourself questioning your skills as a leader and owner. It becomes especially frustrating when you have to spend your valuable time and energy working out the best way to performance manage people out of your business (which is a far more respectful way to think about 'getting rid of' the people who are your liabilities).

If you can identify the issue before the end of someone's probation period, that is ideal. You may lose a few thousand dollars in wages and training, but it is better than hiring the wrong person and realising this after they have passed their probation. You don't want these people to step up—you want them to step out, and step onwards and into the right role for them.

While this person may not be right for your business, they may be a great asset for another business — it's just that the fit isn't right with your business. Perhaps they will be feeling frustrated with themselves for not meeting expectations or for struggling with tasks that others find easy. This can create anxiety about their job security or future prospects within the business. They might worry about the potential repercussions of their underperformance, such as negative evaluations, disciplinary actions or even termination.

The pressure to perform well despite their shortcomings can lead to increased stress levels. They may feel overwhelmed by the demands of the job and the expectations placed upon them by their managers, colleagues or themselves. This can create self-doubt and low self-esteem. They may also feel a sense of guilt or remorse for not living up to the expectations of you — their boss — and so they might feel isolated or ostracised from other people. Often, when the fit isn't right for you, the fit isn't right for them either.

Heracles and Hydra

In Greek mythology, the Lernaean Hydra is a multi-headed serpent, a monster that lives in the swamps of Lerna.

One of Heracles' tasks, set by King Eurystheus, was to slay the Hydra. The Hydra was a monstrous creature with multiple heads, and if one head was cut off, two more would grow in its place. Heracles set out to complete this task with the help of his nephew Iolaus.

As Heracles and Iolaus confronted the Hydra, Heracles quickly realised the challenge ahead. Each time he severed one of the Hydra's heads, two more would sprout in its place. It seemed like an impossible task.

However, Heracles and Iolaus devised a strategy. While Heracles would continue to cut off the heads, Iolaus used a torch to cauterise the neck stumps before new heads could grow. This way, they prevented the Hydra from regenerating more heads. With this combined effort, Heracles and Iolaus managed to defeat the Hydra.

The parable of the Hydra demonstrates several lessons about having the right people in the right jobs.

When working together with the key people in your business to hire new people, you need to ensure you have the right systems in place. And if you don't, you need to address this straight away rather than 'take your eye off the ball' after the hiring process is complete and you move on to the next task.

If I hire someone and, after their probation period is over, they start to act in ways that do not match the values of my business, I often say to myself, 'I have created a Hydra. A monster!' If you don't sort out the wrong people in your business, these people will cause more issues and the number of issues you are dealing with will continue to grow, like the Hydra's heads.

When people who are not suited for a particular role remain in their position, it can create a ripple effect within the business. Their presence may lead competent people to doubt their own abilities and question whether they are in the right role or environment. This can trigger a cascade of people issues, such as decreased morale, increased turnover and diminished productivity. Essentially, retaining the wrong people can sow seeds of doubt and dissatisfaction among the right people, affecting overall performance.

It's essential for business effectiveness and people's morale to address mismatches between people and their roles. When it becomes clear that a hiring decision hasn't had the anticipated best fit, it's important to acknowledge this reality and take swift, decisive action. This involves collaborating closely with your Iolaus (manager) and leveraging HR support to facilitate the respectful and professional exit of people who are not the right fit for the business.

Better still, learning to hire better can save a lot of time, money and energy.

Businesses with 'the right fit' in mind when they hire

Businesses need to commit to hiring the right people if they want to thrive. Here are two recognisable examples of businesses that have found ways to hire wisely:

- **Patagonia** is an outdoor clothing and gear business renowned for hiring people who are not only skilled in their roles but also passionate about environmental and social responsibility. It is committed to hiring people who share the same values, which has contributed to Patagonia's reputation as a socially and environmentally conscious brand.

- **Lush** is a cosmetics business known for hiring people who are passionate about natural and ethical products. Lush's commitment to hiring people who align with the business's values in an authentic way has helped it to maintain a loyal customer base.

Small to medium-sized businesses looking to hire the right people

The following real-life and lived-in examples come from some of the people I've had the privilege to work with and who have been willing to share their hiring experiences. I asked them the question: 'When hiring new people, what methods or techniques do you use to identify their passion for the job or industry?' Here are some of the answers I received.

- **Kate Save, Be Fit Food:** 'We want to know "who you really are" as humans, not just as a workplace.'

- **Wes Blundy, Curvy:** 'You have an extensive Google form that asks lots of questions to identify who you are.'

- **Scott Orpin, MEGT:** 'Just ask them why this job given all the jobs they could go for.'

- **Fiona Anchal, Wholesome Bellies:** 'I recruit based on — is it passion first or is it just for the $$ or a means to an end.'

- **Annika Launay, PDPR Marketing + Creative:** 'Start the dialogue with non-work-related questions to get a general sense of the person.'

- **Kate Winter, Champion Web:** 'Their proactiveness and commitment in conversations.'

- **Liberte Guthrie, Liberte Property & Crossroad Developments:** 'Interviewing for behaviour.'

- **Angus Nicol, Black Market Coffee:** 'Casual chat in the work environment, talk about travel and their personal hobbies.'

- **Ali Koschel, Hunter New England and Central Coast Primary Health Network (HNECC PHN):** 'In the interview process, we focus on values and passion not just the skills they have.'

- **Tina Tower, Her Empire Builder:** 'It is a long process where we have interviews with multiple people and personality profile tools.'

- **Sam Mathers, Fitter Futures:** 'It starts with a coffee, asking questions about their passions and why they want to work here.'

- **Nicole Bryant, The Macro Group:** 'You do a values screen, quiz them about values and passions.'

- **Jane Save, The Save Group:** 'Hire to core values, how they care for customers and do they feel passionate about it.'

Actions

To create a business with passionate people, you may need to change how you hire. Look for diverse perspectives, and focus on finding people who show real excitement for the job and share your business's values.

These four actions can help you build a team that's both diverse and driven, setting the stage for success and growth.

#1. Hire less people who are 'like you'

Often, we are attracted to people that have similar personalities to us. We can relate to them, and we understand the way they speak, their tone of voice and their body language. We resonate with that familiarity. Comforting as this may seem, this is not a good attraction strategy to get the right people in the right job. One of the biggest mistakes that I've made in business is to hire people like me.

Many times, I have entered into an interview process with one of my managers and I have unconsciously leaned towards the candidate who has a similar personality to me rather than the candidate with the right expertise and experience.

One clear example in the corporate world was hiring an executive assistant for myself. I had my HR manager in the interview process there to support me.

We were interviewing three people. The first person did not have much experience but had a great personality. The second person was the opposite. She had a lot of experience but seemed very quiet, and I got short responses and not much engagement. The third person was not available for three months, which did not suit me.

The HR manager suggested the second person. He highlighted to me that we needed someone to follow instructions and did not need a 'bigger' personality. I overturned his insight and hired the first person.

In the back of my mind, during the interview, I had already started to visualise them in the role and how great they were going to be. However, hiring someone similar to you is often the wrong answer when you are not looking at the other attributes that are necessary for them to do that job and leads to the wrong person in the right job in your business.

In finding the right person for a job, it's key to look for certain traits and skills that match what the job needs. This means testing people to see if they have what it takes to do the job well. But sometimes, someone who seems very different from you or others in the team might actually be the best fit for the job. That's because having different perspectives and experiences can bring new ideas and energy to the business.

Even though a person might not seem like the obvious choice at first, they could still be great for the job if they have the right skills and attitude. It's important to keep an open mind and consider all kinds of people to find the best fit for the role and the team.

The short story in this case is that it did not work out so well. The candidate I chose, against my HR manager's advice, had a great personality and was engaging at first. However, she was not great at taking and following instructions, as the HR manager had anticipated. And after three months, she was complaining about the workload (and about me) to others. I should have listened to my HR manager. In this instance, at least we caught the problem within the probation period.

I have made many of these mistakes in my small-to-medium businesses over the last 21 years or so. I have realised that most of the time when I am making these mistakes, I am in a hurry and I am managing too many projects and tasks, or I am reacting in a panic to someone resigning from their job and not honouring their notice period. I make this mistake when I start to feel desperate. And then I rush and hire the wrong person.

And when I have done that more than once, I get angry at myself. 'Why are you not learning?', I ask myself. 'Why are you attracted to personalities rather than listening to your expert people — like your HR manager?'

In my wellness business, which I ran for over a decade, I did this many times. When I first started it in 2012, I was unaware that the industry consisted of younger women in their twenties who work differently to me. I grew up not having any work-life balance and worked even when I was unwell. In those early years, I hired many people thinking they will have similar values and relate to the vision I was outlining.

However, in the wellness industry, different age groups often have different values and take a different approach to their work. Take, for example, a young woman in her twenties working in wellness compared to a manager in their forties (like me). The younger woman might really value having a good balance between work and personal life. She might want flexibility in her schedule to take care of herself and grow outside of work. But as the owner and leader at the time, I had a different view. I grew up in an ethnic family who valued working hard as the most important thing, even if it meant sacrificing personal time, so my values and my vision did not align so well with the younger people in the industry at that time. My employees were into the new, holistic ways of staying healthy, like mindfulness and sustainable living. But I was caught up in more traditional methods of efficiency that I had known for years and which in my mind equated to how I should approach the wellness industry.

Some of the people I hired at the time did not end up being a good fit. They seemed to have completely different values to me. I had put a lot of trust in them and when it did not work, it was heart-breaking.

One example from this business was Anne, a woman in her mid-twenties who had a similar personality to me. The hiring manager pointed out that during the reference check process, one of the referees had highlighted that Anne operated very independently of group decisions. I was desperate to put someone in that position so despite this warning sign, I hired her... only to find out a few months later that I had made a mistake. The person I had hired did not match well to their position description. If I had listened to my manager, we would have hired the right person in the first place. And they never said 'I told you so', which made it worse. These have been expensive and humbling experiences.

As you are reading this, is it resonating? Can you relate to this yourself or see how this may resonate for some of the key people in your business?

As business leaders and owners, you want to be able to understand how the person that you are interviewing fits into the job description and you want to evaluate their interview performance and relevant qualifications and experiences with as few emotions as possible so that you can find the right person for the right job.

In today's business environment, success is based on the dedication and passion of your people. Hiring people who are passionate about their work is a game-changer for any business, especially when you are looking for people to step up.

You don't need to hire another 'you'. You need to focus on hiring the right person for the job!

#2. Choose passionate people

Dispassionate = Disengaged

I believe when people are dispassionate about their work, they are disengaged. And the opposite is true. If a person is passionate about their work, they are more engaged.

Engaged people are not only passionate but they are committed and motivated, which drives productivity and innovation. Most business leaders and owners find it difficult to create more passionate and engaged people, and that is what you need.

Gallup, a research and analytics firm, has conducted extensive studies on the issue of disengagement for many years. According to Gallup data from 2022, only 32 per cent of US workers were engaged in their jobs at that time, while 18 per cent of people were actively disengaged.

An engagement level of 32 per cent is alarmingly low when you are trying to grow your business as you need engaged and passionate people to do their jobs well and make your business successful.

Actively disengaged people are not just dispassionate, they are unproductive and can often be disruptive too, spreading negativity and dissatisfaction among your people. As the saying goes, one bad apple spoils the cart.

The reasons for disengagement

When we as business leaders and owners don't recognise and value our people, there is a decline in engagement. People who are wrong for the job, feel undervalued or believe they are unappreciated are more likely to become disengaged.

A lack of opportunities for skill development and career advancement can also lead to disengagement. People who feel that their careers are 'not going anywhere' are more likely to become disengaged.

Managers play a large role in hiring passionate and engaged people, but they can often be the main reason that people become dispassionate and disengaged with their work — and eventually leave the business.

Why you need passionate people in your business

Passionate and engaged people have intrinsic motivation, which they bring to their work. *Intrinsic motivation* refers to the internal drive or motivation that comes from within an individual rather than from external rewards or pressures.

Passionate and engaged people are driven by a genuine love for what they do. Passion in their life is like fuel or electricity to a car.

Passionate and engaged people also tend to be more productive. Their motivation leads to more focus and efficiency, which impacts profit due to their increased productivity. Passionate and engaged people are not only more productive in their own work but they encourage other people in the people to be passionate and engaged too, which leads to further productivity.

Efficiency is another advantage of passionate and engaged people. Their passion often leads them to explore innovative ways of doing things, streamline processes and find different ways to solve challenges. They are more likely to think creatively and explore new possibilities. Their willingness to push boundaries and embrace challenges can inspire a culture of innovation within the business.

Passionate and engaged people more openly collaborate and share ideas with other people. They are eager to share their passion for their work so they inspire and uplift the people around them, making the business into a culture that is a lot more collaborative. They are more likely to go the 'extra mile' to satisfy and get a 'wow' from customers/clients.

Passionate and engaged people are enthusiastic and, as a result, they have a magnetic effect, inspiring other people to engage more deeply with their own roles.

Passionate and engaged people also contribute to positive brand reputation for your business.

When faced with challenges, they view them as opportunities to learn and grow rather than roadblocks. This is called a *growth mindset.*

Having people with a growth mindset is a huge asset for any business. Business leaders and owners ideally want to hire someone with a growth mindset.

A growth mindset, as defined by psychologist Carol S Dweck in her research, is a belief system centred around the idea that abilities can be developed through effort and learning. In her book *Mindset: The New Psychology of Success*, Dweck discusses the differences between a growth mindset and a fixed mindset.

A growth mindset and a fixed mindset are two ways of thinking about learning and facing challenges. When someone has a growth mindset, they believe that they can improve and develop their abilities over time through effort and practice. They see challenges as opportunities to learn and grow, rather than as obstacles to avoid. For them, setbacks and failures are seen as valuable learning experiences that help them become better at what they do. People with a growth mindset tend to be more resilient and persistent in the face of difficulties because they believe in their capacity to improve.

Conversely, a fixed mindset is characterised by the belief that one's abilities and intelligence are fixed and cannot change significantly. People with a fixed mindset may shy away from challenges because they fear failure and see it as a reflection of their inherent limitations. They may avoid taking risks or trying new things because they believe that their abilities are predetermined and cannot be developed further. As a result, they may miss out on opportunities for growth and personal development.

Dweck's research has shown that those with a growth mindset tend to be more motivated, persistent and open to new experiences. They are more likely to excel in their personal and professional lives because they believe in the power of effort and practice to improve their skills.

She discussed that people with a growth mindset also seek feedback and learn from others, leading to higher levels of achievement in your business as well as the personal development of the individual.

The cost of not hiring passionate people

The costs of hiring the wrong person can amount to between two and five times the person's salary, depending on the industry you work in. You need to consider all the different costs when working out the cost to your business when the wrong person is hired for the job. I encourage you to run a quick cost analysis.

Talent Partners suggests the following thing to consider:

- **Salary and benefits:** How much money you have paid the wrong hire

- **Severance pay:** How much you may need to pay out to terminate the person's employment

- **Replacement salary:** How much you'll need to pay to the right person (when you find them) to bring them up to speed

- **Training costs for the replacement:** How much you need to pay to train the replacement person

- **Turnover costs:** How much impact the wrong hire has had on the bottom line

- **Re-recruitment costs:** How much money you have had to spend on advertising the job again and conducting further interviews

- **Administrative costs:** How much time has been lost to HR costs and management costs during the rehiring process

When you add up the costs, you may have an extra incentive to hire the right people!

#3. How to hire passionate people

One of the books that really helped me understand how to improve my hiring process is *Topgrading* by Bradford D. Smart. It helped me find people who weren't just good at their jobs but were also really passionate about what they do.

Smart shares a system for hiring and retaining the best talent for the job, not just someone who is capable of doing the job. This book taught me to look for people who are not only skilled but also enthusiastic about the work they'll be doing.

The book also talks about keeping good people once you've hired them. This means creating an environment where people feel valued and have opportunities to grow. By doing this, you can make sure that passionate employees stick around and continue to do great work.

Here are the top five lessons that I took away from the book and applied to my businesses.

Lesson 1: Hire and retain A players

Smart advocates hiring and retaining A players, who are the top 10 per cent of your people in any given role. A players not only perform, but they also help drive the success of the business.

To distinguish A players from B and C players:

- **A players:** These are the top performers in a business. They consistently exceed expectations, take initiative and contribute significantly to your business's success. A players are highly skilled, motivated and driven to excel in their roles. They are the ones who consistently deliver outstanding results and are often seen as leaders within their teams.

- **B players:** B players are solid performers who meet expectations but may not go above and beyond like A players. They are competent in their roles and contribute to the business's goals, but they may lack the drive or ambition to become top performers. B players are reliable and dependable people who do their jobs well but may not demonstrate the same level of initiative or innovation as A players.

- **C players:** C players are people who consistently underperform or fail to meet expectations. They may lack the necessary skills, motivation or attitude to succeed in their roles. C players may require more supervision and guidance to complete tasks, and their performance may negatively impact team morale and productivity. In some cases, C players may not be the right fit for the business and may need to be managed out of the company.

Smart argues that one A player can often outperform multiple B or C players.

In all of my businesses, we now assess people according to A, B or C in the business, especially new hires. This also shows the scope of the new hires and how we can develop them into A players through their career development. I also look at how to retain A players.

To help C players become B players, it's important to provide clear expectations and constructive feedback. Start by identifying areas where improvement is needed and communicate these expectations to the person in a supportive manner. Offer training, resources and mentoring to help them develop the necessary skills and knowledge to succeed in their role. Provide regular feedback and coaching sessions to monitor progress and address any challenges or obstacles they may encounter. By investing in their development and providing the support they need, you can help C players enhance their performance and transition to become solid B players within the business.

To elevate B players to A players, focus on fostering a culture of continuous learning, growth and accountability. Encourage B players to set ambitious goals and challenge themselves to reach new heights in their performance. Provide opportunities for professional development, such as advanced training programs, workshops and mentorship opportunities, to help them expand their skills and capabilities. Empower them to take on leadership roles and initiatives that align with their strengths and interests, allowing them to showcase their potential and drive impact within the business.

If after many months of working in the business, the C players are not showing any movement towards being a B player, then consider how you can motivate them to perform. If that doesn't work, you may need to manage them out of the business to create room for another potential A player.

Lesson 2: Use structured interviews and reference checks to evaluate potential hires

Smart's *Topgrading* methodology is a series of structured interviews and assessments to ensure that only the best people are hired and promoted. A structured way of interviewing people involves asking them specific questions to understand how they've handled situations in the past.

Another important lesson involves looking at a person's whole career history. By seeing what they've achieved in the past and how they've grown, you can tell if they're really passionate about their work or if they're just going through the motions. The *Topgrading* methodology includes a 'chronological in-depth interview' that digs deep into people's past experiences, and the 'career-history interview', which examines people's entire work history. The *Topgrading* process also taught me to check people's references thoroughly, talking to people they've worked with before to get a better idea of what they're like.

As a result of reading Smart's book, I realised that I was rushing the interview process in my hiring process. My managers were also mimicking this behaviour. We were not doing in-depth interviews or conducting detailed reference checks, especially when we were hiring for multiple roles at the same time. As a result of reading *Topgrading*, we adopted longer and deeper interviews and a more thorough assessment process that allowed us to hire better people, and our business was able to get the right people in the right jobs.

Lesson 3: Follow the 90 per cent rule

Businesses ideally need to have at least 90 per cent A players in their business. To achieve this, Smart suggests that businesses conduct regular people assessments and upgrade their people pool by replacing underperformers with top people.

To get to 90 per cent A players was difficult for me. When the leaders and I did the assessment, we were sitting at around 30 per cent A players. Only a third of our team! From there, we focused on doubling that to 60 per cent, with 30 per cent B players and 10 per cent C players. The aim was to keep increasing the number of people we could convert from B players to A players.

Lesson 4: Minimise the cost of 'mis-hires'

Smart highlights the costs associated with hiring and retaining underperformers, or 'mis-hires'. These costs go beyond just salary and benefits and include the morale of your people, lost productivity and the potential for costly mistakes.

It doesn't matter which angle you look at it, hiring the wrong people in your business adds costs to the bottom line. And the less obvious costs in areas such as employee morale are harder to measure and can have an exponential impact when you have the wrong person for the job and you then need to performance manage them.

Performance management involves the process of setting goals, assessing progress and providing feedback to people within a business. It's about ensuring that everyone understands what is expected of them, supporting them in achieving those expectations, and recognising and addressing any areas for improvement.

This typically includes regular check-ins, constructive conversations and performance reviews for growth and development. Effective performance management not only helps people reach their potential but also contributes to the success of the business.

It is important to distinguish between managing people out of the business and performance management for career development. Managing people out of the business typically refers to processes like layoffs or terminations due to redundancy or poor performance. Performance management is aimed at improving output and focuses on developing individual skills, setting goals, providing feedback and offering support to help people succeed in their roles and advance their careers within the organisation.

As a result of poor hiring practices in one of my businesses, we suddenly had 20 per cent turnover in a month! That is right, in a month. This had never happened before. This was a disaster and a result of poor hiring practices, which was a big issue. As a leader and business owner, I had to own this statistic. I noticed people started to worry about their work and if there was something wrong in the culture. New hires were also worried and the rumour that was shared with me was that a number of our 'A' players had started to look for other work.

The action I took with my managers was to conduct exit interviews to find out why people were leaving. Almost all of the people said that the job was a lot more about 'following a process' and did not give them creative freedom. The work we wanted done was actually more process-driven, but we realised we had hired creatively driven people to conduct process-driven work. As a result, we rewrote the position description and readvertised with a new focus.

We also ran workshops with the existing people and shared this reflection. Most of the people were really appreciative of this sharing and were able to adjust their style to fit the work. Some even commented that there was now less pressure to follow the process. We lost a couple more people after that session who realised that the role was not right for them. However, the hiring and retention of A players improved from that time on, and we never lost 20 per cent of our people in a month ever again.

As a business leader and owner, if you have a mass exodus, then dig deeper and get to the root cause of what is occurring and why and what can be done to change and action the top issue. Otherwise, the issue can get out of control and impact your culture, which takes years to build (or rebuild).

Lesson 5: Create a regular people review process

A people review process is one where the performance of all your people is regularly assessed. This process helps identify A players, B players and underperformers. It also addresses career development and succession planning, ensuring that the right people are in the right roles.

I recommend you follow this process each quarter. Put each person into either the A, B or C player category according to the earlier definitions. When you're doing this, you need to look at your people with a fresh set of eyes — which means getting other people involved rather you or a previous manager doing this. If you have a preconception of each person, irrespective of which category they fit in, your categorising may be biased towards or against people, even if only subconsciously.

By looking at this every quarter, you can create a discussion and initiate debate on where your leadership people fit and how they are performing. You can also quickly identify the individuals who have moved from C to B and B to A and who you need to coach or train — and retain!

Other ways to hire passionate people

As well as the invaluable insight I gained from *Topgrading*, I have a few other ideas to help put you on the right path when seeking to hire passionate people.

WRITE PASSION-LED JOB DESCRIPTIONS

Have a position description (PD) that not only looks at the qualifications for the role but also allows you to assess whether they are going to be deeply enthusiastic for the role — which equals to someone who is going to be a passionate person for your business. One way to enhance performance management is by carefully creating PDs that focus on the passion and enthusiasm behind the required experience. For example, instead of simply stating that a person must have three years of marketing experience, the PD could highlight the need for someone who is deeply passionate about storytelling and brand development, with a proven track record of creatively engaging audiences. By framing the experience in terms of passion and purpose, the business not only attracts people who are genuinely interested in the work but also where people are motivated to excel.

I always use the word 'passionate' in a PD and when advertising for a role. I have also used other words such as enthusiastic, dedicated, eager, committed, driven, inspired, excited and energetic in PDs as well. I want to see people's enthusiasm shine through in their cover letter and I want to ensure that they understand that we want passionate people in the business. I am looking for the right people. The A players.

LOOK DEEPER INTO THE COVER LETTER AND CURRICULUM VITAE (CV)

I believe passion trumps qualifications. As long as your people have the necessary qualifications to do the job, passion goes much further towards finding the right people for the job.

When working out a shortlist, look deeper into what people are saying and what examples they are providing in their CV and cover letter. Your people need to have a base of qualifications and experience to be able to do their roles, but you also need to use the interview to find the 'gems' — people that are passionate. Look for where they have gone 'above and beyond' and how they show this on their CV.

ASK THE RIGHT INTERVIEW QUESTIONS

Can you share a project or achievement that you are particularly proud of and passionate about?

What inspired you to pursue a career in this industry?

What gets you excited about work each day?

Tell me about a time when your passion for your work made a significant difference in a project or task?

Training managers to ask the right interview questions is a key component of hiring the right person. They need to ask questions around passion and engagement. They need to find the 'A' players.

CHECK REFERENCES THOROUGHLY

Many CVs now say 'referees upon request'. Request them!

Reference checks are an essential step in the hiring process. I know referees are going to say positive things about the person you want to hire, but you want to know these details nonetheless.

You want to gain valuable insights into a person's suitability for the role. Beyond confirming their professional experiences, reference checks that reveal how their behaviour reflects their passion are key.

Ensure you receive three referees per candidate. My manager or I will ring all the referees provided and ask a question about the candidate's passions and how 'into' things they are. And I ask for examples.

Contacting referees when hiring offers several benefits. Firstly, it provides an opportunity to verify the information provided by the applicant. This helps ensure that the person's qualifications, experience and skills align with what they have claimed. By speaking directly to previous business leaders or owners, hiring people can gain insights into the person's work ethic, performance and reliability.

Secondly, contacting referees allows for a deeper understanding of the person's strengths and areas for development. Referees can offer valuable perspectives on the abilities, communication style and interpersonal skills, which may not be clear from interviews or their CV.

This information can help making a more informed hiring decision and assessing how well the person may fit within the team and business. Moreover, reaching out to referees shows diligence in the hiring process, which can improve your business's reputation and credibility.

WORK OUT IF YOUR VALUES ARE ALIGNED

You want to test the values of your business (refer to Chapter 1) against the person you want to hire and their values. You are mainly checking for what I call any 'red flags' in terms of culture clashes or value clashes.

This is also an important time as a business leader and owner to know the passions of the people you are about to hire. How do you determine these? Well, I am glad you asked!

#4. Using the Passion Model to understand your interviewees' passions

People will always operate and be motivated by things that they are passionate about. When people arrive at an interview, they tell you that they are very passionate about you and your business in order to be successful at the interview. They have 'googled' you and the business.

At the core, however, people are really passionate about the things that they are passionate about rather than you or your business. It is really important to remember that.

To explore this concept more deeply, I created what I call the Passion Model. I developed this model so that I could hire more passionate people in my team. I wanted to hire people that cared. I wanted to understand people and what they were 'into' or passionate about so I could communicate with them easily.

I believe that when you speak to people on what they are passionate about, you cannot stop them talking, even if they are an introvert. And equally, you cannot get people interested in contributing to a conversation if it is on a topic that they are not interested in, even if they are an extrovert.

Let me explain how this model works and how you can build this model into your hiring process.

There are seven areas to the Passion Model: work, mind, money, friends, soul, body and family. You may wish to call each area something slightly different that resonates more with you; the words are interchangeable. For example, mind is the same as learning. Body is the same as health … and so on.

When I started to put this simple but powerful tool together, I realised that as humans we are trying to master everything, rather than a few things. No wonder we are so exhausted!

You can, however, only master three areas out of seven. Trying to master everything is not possible. At best, you will be mediocre in all seven areas.

The Passion Model

I usually set the three areas I want to go deeper into and master for a whole 12 months as I believe mastery takes time.

Using the Passion Model, you can create mastery in three areas of life that you choose by complementing passion with discipline.

Most people I speak to about this model struggle with the areas they cannot master. They often feel guilty for consciously choosing to focus on some areas and not others.

You must choose (consciously!) what three areas you want to master and what you do not, which means you will be mediocre in the areas you don't choose — you may even be terrible in those areas.

So — choose wisely!

Passion without discipline is a waste of time

People speak about passion as being a fleeting thing. It is expected that you are passionate about something for a short period of time, which can often lead to no or short-term results. While passion provides the initial spark of enthusiasm and motivation, discipline is what creates results.

Passion can sound like something you can swap as easily as your clothes. Many people talk about the word as something they desire. It may lead to intense activity but, without discipline, these actions are unlikely to have enough energy or last for enough time to get to the end outcomes you were hoping for.

Discipline brings accountability. When you're disciplined, you set goals, establish routines and hold yourself accountable for your actions. Without this, passion can easily lead to procrastination, distraction or the temptation to give up when faced with challenges.

Discipline helps in skill development. Achieving mastery in any field requires deliberate practice and a commitment to improvement over time. Discipline keeps you on the path of learning, growing and refining your skills, which is essential for turning passion into expertise.

Discipline provides resilience. Pursuing one's passion often involves setbacks, failures and obstacles. Discipline gives you the mental resilience to overcome any challenges and through these difficulties, learn from them and keep moving forward.

While passion is the driving force behind what excites us, discipline is what turns passion into meaningful outcomes. They complement each other, with passion providing the inspiration and enthusiasm and discipline providing the structure and perseverance needed for success.

Without discipline, passions are likely to remain an idea that you are hoping will come true but as the saying goes 'Hope is not a plan'.

When you couple passion and discipline, you create mastery!

When striving to master seven areas of passion, it's important to recognise the limitations of human capacity. While it may seem tempting to master all seven, spreading oneself too thin often results in only achieving a superficial understanding of each area. This phenomenon is often described by the saying 'Jack (or Jill) of all trades, master of none'. In other words, when trying to juggle too many pursuits, people fail to develop deep expertise in an area.

Focusing on mastering three areas of passion allows people to dedicate their time, energy and resources more effectively. By concentrating efforts on a select few areas, people can delve deeply into their chosen passions, gaining an understanding and sharpening their skills.

Anyone that is known for great success, whether they be an athlete or a business person, did not try to do it all. They are focused on what they are good at.

When you think of your passions, I hope you find it helpful to remember that passion without discipline may lead to fleeting and mediocre outcomes.

 Work in the Passion Model

Let's talk about passion at work. What do you mean when people are passionate about their work? As business leaders and owners, you might call work 'business' — but the words are interchangeable.

If you are really passionate about your work, your behaviour in the workplace will align with your work. People that are passionate about work will put their hand up for projects, make the time to stay back after their work is finished and put in extra effort.

They are curious about their work and ask a lot of questions. When people are really passionate about what they do, they are constantly interested in their work. They're thinking about their work, they're doing their work, they're excited to talk about it at a family barbecue and they want to continue to have an impact at work.

On the other hand, when people are not passionate about their work, then the behaviours that you see are people that watch the clock and leave exactly on the dot.

These people don't put their hand up for extra work, they are not curious about their work, they are disinterested, they are not present and are often doing other things when you might be discussing important work.

It's important to have people in our businesses that are passionate about their work. The mistake that a lot of business leaders and owners make is that they expect work to be the number one passion for their people, which is understandably not always the case.

Some of the best people that have worked for me have been those for whom work is not their top passion. But it's often their passion number two, three or four. As business owners and leaders, you need to work out how to tap into people's passions and serve them by giving them things that meet their passion. And in return, you want your people to serve your passion for your work. It is a two-way street.

It's totally okay if work isn't your absolute number one passion in life. For business owners and leaders, work might feel like their baby, something they're super invested in and care about deeply. But for your people, it's normal to have other things they're passionate about too, like hobbies, family or personal goals.

Having different passions outside of work actually brings a lot of good stuff to the table. It means people bring diverse ideas and experiences to their jobs, which can make the business more creative and interesting. Plus, when people are happy and engaged with their work, they can still do an awesome job, even if it's not the thing they're most passionate about.

So, as long as you care about your work and do your best, it's totally fine if it's not your top passion. What matters most is that you feel fulfilled and motivated in what you're doing, whether it's work or something else.

 ## Mind in the Passion Model

The next part of this model I'd like to discuss is mind. Learning and mind are two words that are interchangeable. People with mind as a passion want to keep learning about everything. They have a curiosity about the world around them, a lifelong learning mindset, and they want to continue to learn and grow. I discuss this more in Chapter 5.

If you are passionate about work or business and you are also very passionate about your mind, one of the things you'll find is that you want to learn about things that are related to your work: things that are going to progress your career or business, and progress your or your people's leadership capabilities. You'll want to learn about anything related to your work and business to help it grow.

However, if your mind is something that you're very passionate about and your work is something that you're not very passionate about, you'll find yourself learning about a lot of things unrelated to work, whether it is surfing or basket weaving. Your learning will not necessarily be about work.

One of the common questions I ask when I'm trying to determine if someone is passionate about their mind is whether they buy books and never find the time to read them.

For those people that buy books and don't find the time to read them, they would like mind to be a passion but they do not have the time to do it. However, if mind is a passion, then they will make time to do things related to living the passion of mind, which can include reading.

The desire to have one of your passions come first is not an indicator that your behaviours will align with your passions.

The gap in reality is there because there is a gap in your mind. You want things to be higher in life but in reality, you make no time for them to be higher.

Mind is in my top three passions. As a result, I make time for 10–60 minutes of reading each day and read a lot of books each year. I buy a lot of books, especially at airports. If I have spare time, I read a book with a nice pot of tea. This is one of my favourite things to do in life.

The key is to either have mind as one of your top three passions and make time for it in your life, or to stop buying books and know that it is not a high enough passion for you, so you don't feel guilt around wanting mind to be a higher priority.

 ## Money in the Passion Model

The next part of the model you're going to look at is money. This word is interchangeable with wealth. It is also interchangeable with investment.

For a lot of people, money gives them freedom.

People who are passionate about money tend to do a few things differently. They keep a close eye on what they spend and earn, making sure everything adds up. They set clear goals for their money, like saving up for something special or making sure they have enough for emergencies. They're also good at finding ways to make the most of their money, like cutting back on unnecessary spending or looking for ways to earn extra cash. This careful approach to managing money helps them stick to a budget and reach their financial goals. They can project what they want to earn or what they want their profit margin to be in their current business. And they're very good at working out where they want to be in three years, five years, 10 years and perhaps even longer when it comes to money and wealth.

Sometimes people that are passionate about money appear stingy about money towards other people, but they are mindful and passionate about what they spend. It's their passion. They want to be able to keep as much money as possible. If mind and money are in their top three passions, they will often be reading and learning about how to keep and make more money.

If work and money are in their top three passions, they will want to be clear how their business will lead them to having more money and wealth.

Consider some of the people in your life — is money a passion for them? Maybe some of your family have money as a passion. And maybe you can see where the people in your team may be passionate about money.

They will be the ones that will ask you for a raise or an increase in benefits. They want a clear plan for their careers so they can earn extra money.

As leaders and business owners, it can be easy to judge your people when their passions do not match yours. You may judge people because they are interested in money and you may not be, or vice versa.

I have also had the opportunity to work with business owners who are not really passionate about their business or the 'why' it stands for, but they are really passionate about money. They will find a gap in the marketplace.

And they are very excited about that gap as they believe they can close it and serve that market and, in the process, make a lot of money.

If I ask them if they're really passionate about their product or their service, or whatever widget it is that they're selling, their answer is often no.

Changing incentives to suit the individual may not be possible for all businesses, but it is worth seeing whether you can incentivise people according to their passions.

For example, I have had people that made me rethink my bonus system for people who want to make a lot of money because in return, they then make my business a lot of money. As money is not in my top three passions, this was a revelation for me and got me thinking outside of the box.

When I work with businesses whose salespeople are not performing, I use the Passion Model to work out their passions and see where money fits into their passions. If money is in their top three passions and they have a commission structure, they seem to do well, but they don't do so well if money is not in their top three passions. They are doing the role but not passionately!

FRIENDS Friends in the Passion Model

The next part of the model I want to speak about is friends, a word that is interchangeable with social. Sometimes social media would also fit into that. People that are passionate about friends are the ones that are constantly thinking about their friends.

They're thinking about how to connect with them. They make sure that they send them regular messages, they make sure that they organise time to be able to catch up with them. They remember special occasions in their life. They will be there for you. I have one of these beautiful friends in my life who has been a friend of mine for over 30 years. And although we live in different cities, she will constantly make that effort because friends are in her top three passions.

I will get handmade cards for my birthday and the kids' birthdays, because she knows that all of those things are really important for me. And I feel awful as a friend sometimes but then I have to remind myself that friends isn't in my top three passions. Although I'm a very loyal friend, I don't spend as much time thinking about or doing the work around my friends, but I am present and available to the key friends in my life.

I also don't need to see my friends multiple times a week or every week. I know they are there and I am there for them.

In business, people that are really into friends on social will often be the people that will come up with suggestions on how to connect more with people in the business. They want to create time to connect with people at work.

Their ideas may range from Friday Happy Shirt Day, cake to celebrate people's individual birthdays, social drinks on a Friday night or other things. They want the opportunity to spend time and hang out with each other. For people that are really into social and friends and they're passionate about it, they can't wait for these events. They want to be there and are willing to volunteer at work to connect with other people socially and to create an environment that creates social and work friends.

For others, they are not passionate about friends at work. When social events are planned at work, they might be heard saying things like, 'Great, I've just spent the whole week with you and now you want me to have drinks with you on a Friday night as well. No thanks.' And if they are not saying these things loudly, they may be saying that to themselves. And they will quietly leave the office at the end of the day.

Before planning social events for your team or business, think about what each person enjoys. Some people love socialising, while others might not be as keen. If socialising isn't one of their top passions, they might not want to attend the events. It's important to understand and respect every-one's preferences to make sure everyone feels included and comfortable.

 ## Soul in the Passion Model

The next area of the Passion Model is soul. Soul is a word that sometimes people get very confused about and this word can be interchanged with religion, philosophies and values.

Behaviours that you might see around soul may include giving away some of your time for a particular charity, helping out at your kids' school or donating money to a particular cause that is very meaningful to you.

You make some time to meditate or pray (whatever your belief system is). Remember that you will make the time to do the things you are passionate about. People who desire soul to be higher but know it is not one of their top passions may never find the time to meditate.

I have had various conversations with people over the years who believe that soul or religion is a top passion for them. They will tell me (irrespective of their religious beliefs) that soul is a passion for them and they make time to go to their place of worship daily or weekly.

However, if you go to these places to bond with others, then your deeper behaviour when examined may actually be friends or social. This is a challenging perspective I know but I want you to be clear not only about your passions but also those of your people.

Consider another example. If you volunteer at one of your kids' school barbecues or fundraisers, ask yourself, 'Am I doing it because it's feeding my soul? Am I doing it to make some friends for myself and my children? Or am I doing it really for my family to be able to connect there?' All of the reasons are valid, but you want to ensure that you understand the deeper passion at work here.

When you understand *why* you do what you do, then decision-making becomes easier.

You want to be able to live according to your passions, not the passions of others.

I've known people that have refused to work for certain businesses because of what that business stands for or the products they are producing. For some people, it really bothers them that they might be working for a mining, tobacco, alcohol or plastics business, because for them that doesn't resonate with their soul. Others do not mind as it does not cause any internal conflicts between the values of the business and their own values. And that's not to say that people who work for a tobacco business have no soul. The key point is that you will weigh up your values in a very different way if soul is a passion for you. It's all about living according to your passions.

 ## Body in the Passion Model

The next area on the Passion Model I would like to discuss is body. This word is interchangeable with health.

It's equally important to be able to look at body and health from an internal perspective and make sure that you are healthy on the inside as well as outside. Often body and health only seem to focus on what you look like or what you weigh.

I want to share a personal experience with you. For many years, one of the things that I had always wished for was to be a dress size smaller. And for that I knew I needed to exercise more and I needed to eat better and eat less. I needed to be able to say no to and refuse extra food or drinks when they were offered to me.

I find saying no to seconds for food challenging, especially when it is delicious!

My desire was to be a dress size less but my behaviour was to be able to eat and drink what I liked and then I would feel awful and also feel shame for over indulging. This pattern was repeated for years if not decades. I would take out what I called my 'invisible whip' and would whip myself with words, telling myself how bad I was for not being able to resist a second helping of food. This was also self-destructive for my self-esteem.

When I present this part of the model, the question I want to ask you is, 'Was body and health a passion and goal for you this year? Was this going to be your year to get fitter, faster, lose weight or get more toned?' Many of you might invisibly put your hand up to this question.

And hand on your heart (be true to yourself) how many of you had the same goal last year?

Keep your hand up. And how many of you had the same goal the year before that?

If you were honest with yourself and found that invisible hand was still in the air, it is unlikely you are going to make that goal and passion this year. And the reason is because you have this desire to do something but, again, your behaviours do not match your desire.

The decision I really had to make was do I want to put body into my top three passions or not? This was hard as I did want to, but my top three passions are work, family and mind, and I did not want to compromise on any of these.

I didn't want body and health to be last place on the list in the Passion Model, but at the same time I realised it was not going to make the top three. As a result, I left it at number four knowing that I may not be able to master this passion, which may equate to never being a dress size smaller. What I did decide to stop though was the way I used the invisible whip to facilitate the horrific love-hate relationship that I had developed around my body, and how I treated it with my mind and my ego.

One of the things I say to leaders and business owners is if it's in your top three, then live according to those passions. People that are really passionate about their body often arrive at speaking engagements with some of their own snacks, just in case there are only really unhealthy options available. They will get up and exercise irrespective of the weather, whether it's rain, hail or shine.

They will make sure that they're setting goals for their body that they're also going to be able to achieve. I have a couple of friends who will exercise every single day, sometimes even twice a day, irrespective of the weather, irrespective of whether they are on planes, irrespective of whether they are in other countries. That's somebody who's really committed to their body and health and who places body and health as their number one passion (or certainly in the top three).

An amazing woman became one of the leaders in my businesses. And when I interviewed her and talked about this model with her, one of the things that came out was that her body and health was her number one passion. And work was number two. As a business owner, I decided that I would pay for her membership to the best gym in the city, which was $1500 a year. And I paid for that membership for the whole four years that she was with me in the business. And she loved me for it!

We very openly discussed that it was really important for me as a business owner to feed her passion. And equally, it was really important for her to feed my passion, which is work (my number one passion). As business leaders and owners, we need to build this narrative into the interview process and beyond that into incentives as part of our retention strategy. By tapping into her passion and building an incentive out of it, I engaged her effectively into her role.

Family in the Passion Model

The last part of the model I want to speak about is family. I've deliberately left this to last. In my experience, if I ask, 'Who's passionate about their family?' almost everyone says yes, and that family is in their top three passions. And then, when I ask the question, 'How many of you spend as much time thinking about family as you do your work? And how many of you actually spend as much time with your family as you do at work?', people realise that they may not spend eight or nine hours of quality time a day with their family, which can make them question where their priorities actually lie.

Where does your energy lie? To understand this more fully, it may help to examine the behaviours of someone who is passionate about their family.

People that are very passionate about their family are the ones that are constantly thinking about them. They are always thinking, 'How can I help them; how can I help them grow? What do I need to do around what they need to eat? What do I need to do around the kids' education? What conversations do I want to have? What experiences do I want to create?' And so on. The list is long.

Family is my number two passion and I spend a lot of time thinking about these questions. As a woman, and more importantly as an ethnic woman who was taught to sacrifice herself for her family, I find it hard to say that my passion for work is higher than my passion for family. It is not that I would not take a bullet for my kids and husband, it is that I don't think about them as much as I do about work.

People that don't have family in their top three passions still love their family. It's important not to confuse passion and love, which sometimes seems interchangeable but is actually very different.

For people whose family is their top passion, they make sure to spend quality time with their loved ones whenever they can. They plan activities together and always think about what's best for their family. Even though they have other things to do, they never forget the importance of family time and try to make it a regular part of their lives. They may not always talk about their family, but their actions show how much they care about them.

One of my clients who's got older children talks about the fact that their family was in his top three passions when the kids were younger, but as they have become adults and went about their separate lives, that became less of a focus and his family has come down in his list of passions and is no longer in his top three.

The Passion Model in action

I want to share an example of a person that ended up working for me for five years. Their number one passion was also work and so I knew that they wanted to work and they also asked me if I had a ladder they could climb in their career. They understood what needed to be done to reach the manager's position from the time they started. We created a career plan for her so she could see which level she was working in at all times. Most people got to the management role within four or five years. She got there in two!

In another example, I hired a leader who worked for me for four years in one of my businesses. She had money as a number one passion and for her that gave her freedom. She had shared with me that her family had historical issues around money and money beliefs growing up. This upbringing made her feel that she did not want to experience that level of poverty or as close to as she got ever again. She wanted to work on being financially independent on her yearly pay. She wanted to make sure that she had financial freedom, which included following rigorous budgets and having investment properties.

When I shared the Passion Model with her in the interview and asked about her top three passions, I explained to her that I did not expect my leaders to have work as their top passion. She felt she got permission to share with me that money was her number one passion.

She 'lit up' talking about money. She spoke about the fact that she likes knowing what the business is making in revenue and profit. She asked me excellent questions about my desired revenue and profit. She also wanted to understand if her contract would give her the opportunity to make more money if she exceeded her targets.

I loved these questions. I realised that if there was no 'ceiling' on what she could earn, she would continue to grow in this role. We spoke about having a base salary and a bonus system that we could monitor on a monthly basis. Her questions also helped me redesign my incentive program for leaders.

As you know, good leadership is about knowing yourself first. You want to understand your passions as they stand now.

Before you move on to working on how you build the Passion Model into interviews and incentivising your people, take a moment and get a piece of paper so you can evaluate your own passions.

Here's a step-by-step process to follow:

1. Take a sheet of paper and draw a vertical column.

2. Write down the numbers 1 to 7 in the column, representing your passions from most to least.

Then, identify your passions:

1. Start by reflecting on how you currently spend your time and what you think about most.

2. Write down the area that you engage with the most as your number one passion.

3. Then, identify the next most prominent area in your life and write it down as your number two passion.

4. Continue this process until you've ranked all seven passions, with your least engaged area as number seven.

Then, organise your passions:

1. Revisit your list and find the bottom two passions (number six and number seven).

2. The one you engage with slightly more becomes your number four passion.

3. The remaining one becomes your number five passion.

By following these steps, you'll have a clearer understanding of what your current passions in life are.

If you want to change your passions, you are able to do that but it is more than just moving them around in a different order on a piece of paper. Your behaviours have to align with your passions too.

And now let us get to how to use it with your people...

Using the Passion Model in interviews

In interviews, I suggest that you share the model, quickly explain it and share examples of how you have leaders that have different passions and how this helps your business work. Ask the candidate to quickly fill out their passions by putting 1 though to 7 on it and then and share it with you.

During interviews, introducing the Passion Model swiftly can provide valuable insights into their passions. You could also share examples of leaders within the business who show different passions and how these passions contribute to business success.

Encouraging people to quickly rank their passions from 1 to 7 shows self-reflection and transparency. This approach prompts people's interests, values, and potential alignment with the business culture and objectives.

The people that openly share with you in the interview knowing you are the business leader and owner not only know their passions but it is an indication that they know who they are and are able to communicate this with you.

For the others who do not know what their passions are or your instinct tells you are making up the passions, it gives you an insight into how honest they are at communicating, or it suggests they do not know themselves.

Although this is not a 'foolproof' methodology, it is a great tool to use as one of the many questions you have prepared for an interview.

Understanding your people's passions can provide insights into their behaviours both inside and outside of work.

Slowing down the hiring process allows for more careful consideration and better decision-making when it comes to selecting the right people. While the phrase 'hire fast and fire faster' may suggest fixing a problem fast, rushing through hiring can lead to costly mistakes and mismatches.

By taking the time to thoroughly assess a person's skills, experience and passions, business leaders and owners can make more informed hiring choices that are more likely to result in long-term success.

Using the Passion Model to incentivise and reward your people

The Passion Model can be helpful from an incentive, reward and retention perspective as well as during the hiring process. For example, if you have a budget of $250 for a yearly Christmas gift for each of your people, don't just give a hamper with a ham or turkey. Give them something they are passionate about, such as a massage voucher if Body is a passion, or a book voucher if they love reading and Mind is one of their passions.

My Passion Model for 2024

This does not need to mean anything to anyone else but just to me. It is taking my top three passions of work, family and mind and then lower ones and taking images that inspire me to create this.

I also have certain words that become my mantra for the year such as calm and connected. In 2024 it is focus.

Case study: Basecamp

An example of a small to medium-sized business that strategically slowed down its hiring process to ensure the recruitment of top-tier talent is Basecamp, a project management and team collaboration software business founded by Jason Fried and David Heinemeier Hansson.

Basecamp has long been recognised for its commitment to creating a unique and positive workplace culture. In their book *Rework*, the founders shared their unconventional approach to hiring, emphasising quality over speed.

The business deliberately slowed down its hiring process to focus on finding people who not only had the necessary skills but also aligned with the business's values.

One of the key parts of Basecamp's hiring strategy is the detailed evaluation of people based on their cultural fit.

The business values autonomy, a calm work environment and a strong commitment to work-life balance. Instead of rushing through the hiring process, Basecamp ensures that people understand and resonate with these values.

This involves an assessment of cultural alignment during interviews and even a trial period where people work on actual projects before a final hiring decision is made.

By taking the time to understand people on a deeper level, Basecamp aims to avoid making decisions that could lead to mismatched hires. This approach also allows the business to assess people not just in terms of their technical skills but also on their ability to thrive in Basecamp's unique work culture.

The deliberate pace in hiring has paid off for Basecamp. The business has a team of talented people who not only excel in their roles but also contribute to the collaborative atmosphere.

Basecamp's emphasis on quality over quantity in hiring aligns with the philosophy that a team of highly skilled and culturally aligned people can outperform a larger team with less cohesion.

Basecamp's commitment to a deliberate hiring process has become a case study for other companies seeking to build effective teams and hire the right people.

Reflections

Before diving into the questions that follow, ensure you have a journal and a pen within reach to capture your thoughts. Refer to Chapter 1 if you need a reminder on how to create the ideal setting for these reflections about your business. Consider the questions and journal your answers. Remember, you may also like to ask the people in your business to reflect on the same questions.

The questions are broken down into several sections. Separating the questions into distinct areas allows for a more structured and focused approach to addressing each aspect of recruiting passionate people. By breaking down the discussion into specific topics, we can go deeper into each area, explore relevant questions, and develop actionable insights and strategies. This approach facilitates a more detailed way of looking at important aspects. Additionally, the discussion into separate sections helps maintain clarity and coherence, making it easier for you to track progress and identify areas for further exploration or improvement.

Hiring the wrong person:

- Have you hired the wrong person before for a job?

- Have there been instances where you felt the fit wasn't quite right with someone you brought on board?

- Do you know how much the mis-hire cost you? Multiply over a year.

- What were your learnings?

Having disengaged and dispassionate people:

- What percentage of your people do you think are disengaged or dispassionate?

- Have you had a chance to assess the level of engagement among your team members and identify any trends?

- What are your passions as a business leader and owner?

Creating a vision board:

- Have you created a vision board?

- Do you know the top three passions of ALL your key people?

- Are your incentives for your people as per their passions?

- Thinking about motivation, have we explored aligning incentives with the individual passions of your team members?

Using the Passion Model:

- How will you incorporate the Passion Model into interviews?

- What are your top three passions (from the Passion Model), and how are you communicating those passions to your team?

- What passions do you believe are key to the success of your team?

Assessing your team's skills:

- What specific skills are lacking in your team?

- Looking at our team's skill set, do you see any specific areas where your business might be lacking, and how can you address those gaps?

Attracting the right people:

- What part of your business culture is important for people to understand?

- What do you need to do to find people who share your passion?

Keeping the right people:

- What can you do to motivate people beyond financial incentives?

- What learning and development opportunities would help you with getting the right people?

- What can you do to identify people with great problem-solving skills?

- What can you do to tailor your incentives to resonate with the passions of potential people?

Summary

In the journey of building and leading businesses over the past two decades, one of my key learnings has been that hiring people like myself is a pitfall. It's a mistake that I have made both in the corporate area as well as in my small to medium-sized businesses. This has been an expensive and painful journey.

The tendency to be attracted to personalities similar to our own, especially in moments of desperation, often leads to the wrong person in the right job or the right person in the wrong job. Both are important to get right.

Understanding the need for diversity, not just in terms of demographics but also in personalities, is something that every business leader and owner must address.

My other key learning has been that passion is a key strategy, and moving from disengagement to engagement begins with recognising the importance of passionate people. The global statistics on disengagement irrespective of industry show the importance for business leaders and owners to prioritise passion in their hiring strategies.

I hope the introduction of the Passion Model will provide you with a strategy to look through a new lens from which to assess and understand people you want to bring in and retain in your business.

Passionate and engaged people contribute significantly to the success of a business. They bring productivity, innovation and a positive culture, and they create a ripple effect that can influence others.

Understanding the costs of mis-hires and actively working to avoid them is not just a financial strategy but crucial in maintaining a healthy business culture.

Strategies for hiring passionate people go beyond traditional approaches. Implementing the insights from the *Topgrading* methodology, conducting thorough reference checks and aligning with your values are critical steps in ensuring the right fit.

CHAPTER 3
PLAN A, B AND C

Coaching emerging leaders and developing your succession plan

Succession planning is a powerful tool for retaining key people.

People are more likely to stay with a business that offers clear paths for career advancement. Succession planning shows a commitment to people development and growth. People can then see a future for themselves within the business.

Succession planning identifies skills gaps within the business and provides a roadmap for people to get the necessary skills and competencies to move up the ladder. Investing in your people's training and development not only prepares them for future roles but also improves their current performance. When people know they are being considered for future leadership positions, they tend to be more engaged, committed and aligned with the business's goals.

Succession planning is used by businesses where there is a change of ownership. A succession plan involves identifying internal employees who would like a career advancement and training them to assume new roles within the company. Succession planning ensures that business knowledge is passed down from one person to the next. This knowledge retention is key to a business's success now and in the future. Senior managers and people may be more willing to stay on as mentors and advisors, knowing that their expertise is valued and needed.

Succession plans only work if companies take the steps necessary to prepare. One of the mistakes that I have made when running my own businesses is not getting the succession plan right, mainly due to a lack of planning, a lack of focus and what I call the 'busyness disease' — in other words, getting so busy in the present that we forget about what we need to do to plan for our long-term future success. This is where succession planning comes in. Making time for a succession plan is essential for the continuity of the business.

When businesses are starting to grow and scale, it is easy to become so busy with the hiring process, and with making sure that the delivery of the business's products and services is occurring on time, that you neglect to put a really good succession plan into place — which soon starts to show in the business's output.

If one of your key people resigns, this can feel really stressful and you may have a few sleepless nights wondering what you've done wrong and why you hadn't noticed they were a 'flight risk'. This feeling becomes even worse if you don't have someone in the team who is a natural successor to this key person.

If you don't know why your key people are leaving, it can leave you feeling as if you don't have your finger on the pulse of the people in your team. Maybe you're not spending enough time with them, or perhaps they weren't the right person for the right job and you haven't yet figured that out (refer to Chapter 2).

As your business starts to grow from one or two people to many people, it becomes critical to be able to onboard each person properly, making sure they are well trained and ensuring that they are able to service your clients and work to the best of their abilities. With succession planning and when you have the right people for the right job, you can work towards retaining key people but also have a solution in place if they naturally move on to another role.

Succession planning for business confidence

One of the things that I've learned the hard way has been to ensure that not only do I have a Plan A in place, but that I also have a Plan B ready to replace Plan A. And then, that I also have a Plan C that can replace Plan B.

If you have already earmarked people to move up a level on the ladder, you can ensure that succession planning works. It's a far better option than fumbling around and rushing to replace people and then making the wrong choice (as discussed in Chapter 2).

This strategy does require extra time, energy, money and investment as a business leader and owner to budget for these changes in the business, but the return is well worth the effort as succession planning takes away a lot of worries and concerns while you're leading and growing your business.

The extra costs are to ensure that the person earmarked for progress is able to develop the competencies, capabilities, skills and, more importantly, the confidence for them to step into person A's role as and when needed. You then need to repeat that process ready for person C to step into person B's role when the time comes.

Most of the time, you won't have an exact timeline of when person A may leave, and some business owners may not agree with the extra cost coming in advance of succession planning being put into action.

You can test whether person B has the skills to do the role of person A by asking them to step up in the absence of person A (who may be on annual leave, for example). This temporary secondment gives person B some confidence if they perform the more senior role successfully or it may provide you and person B with an opportunity to do additional training or receive extra coaching.

The alternative to not having such succession plans in place for people puts too much risk on you being able to run your business with confidence while maintaining business continuity. The risk of disruption is always there at the slightest shift in your team.

The importance of having a Plan B ... and even a Plan C

Ingrid runs an accounting business with 12 employees. She has decided that one of her managers, Sam, will take over the business when she retires. However, Sam gets ill and decides not to take over Ingrid's business as planned. In fact, he decides to leave the business to prioritise his health. This leaves Ingrid with no choice but to keep working in the business until she can find another suitable candidate to run the business—or she may even have to close down the business. Even with a succession plan in place (Plan A, where Sam takes over the business), Ingrid is faced with the scenario where she actually needed a Plan B in place—and who knows, maybe even a Plan C.

Many small-to-medium businesses today cannot name a successor to their business leader or owner should the need arise. Furthermore, succession planning statistics show that the vast majority of US small businesses, even long-standing, successful ones, are facing a critical juncture. According to small business platform Teamshares, nearly two-thirds of small business owners in the US plan to retire in the next two years without a solid succession plan in place.

Many advisors say that succession planning should be started five years before the business leader or owner plans to retire. In reality, however, business owners often want to sell the business when the business owner is feeling 'burnt out' and has had enough, according to brokerage firm Link Business.

In such instances, a business owner may not be able to get the full value of their business during the exit process. Other risks of not having a succession plan in place include potential successors leaving due to lack of transparency, putting the business at risk; increased difficulty in obtaining financing; a shortage of the right people; loss of knowledge with the people that leave; and low morale in the remaining team.

Being proactive ensures that the right people are going to step up and that they have enough knowledge and experience to take on the full range of responsibilities, and that in advance of this transition they can build their leadership abilities in readiness. This also gives a business owner additional options when exiting a business, as the people in their succession plan may also be the right people to buy the business, making for a smooth business exit process.

Having good succession planning in place allows for a smooth transition of leadership and people, promotes business stability and continuity, enhances people development prospects and reduces the risks associated with leadership gaps.

Lao's trees

Once in a small village there lived a wise elder named Lao. Lao was known for his forward thinking and guidance. He used storytelling as a way of imparting valuable lessons.

His favourite saying was, 'The best time to plant a tree was 20 years ago and the second best time is today.'

The village had fertile soil and enough rainfall, making it an ideal place for farming. However, Lao was not only concerned with the immediate needs of the village but also with its long-term future.

One of the villagers explained to Lao, 'Our crops are flourishing and the village is thriving. We have more than enough to eat and sell. Why do you keep talking about planting more trees?'

Lao shared a story in reply: 'One of our neighbouring villages was much like ours. They enjoyed great harvests for many years. However, there came a time when their soil began to erode and their crops withered and their village faced the threat of becoming unliveable.

'The villagers remembered the wisdom of planting trees. They had failed to do so in the past. They decided to act swiftly. They planted trees along the riverbanks to prevent further erosion and dug wells to ensure a stable water supply. They worked diligently until the village flourished.'

The villager realised that while the village was thriving today, there was no guarantee that the same abundance would last forever and it was important to think about the future. So the villagers began planting trees to safeguard the land, invested in education and training for their youth, and initiated succession planning to ensure the continuity of their community.

The point of sharing Lao's parable is that despite your business flourishing now with the right people, things can change quickly when a couple of your key people leave suddenly. Planting the right people (like the trees) avoids the unplanned-for erosion of your business as other people can quickly replace the people that have left with some additional support and training.

Succession planning successes and failures

Succession planning done well can be transformative for a business. Here are just a few recognisable examples of succession plan successes and failures from the business world:

- **McDonald's.** Ray Kroc, the visionary behind the global success of McDonald's, saw the importance of succession planning. Kroc was not just focused on his own role as the business leader and owner, but on developing a team of talented people within the business. He identified key people who showed potential and actively worked to nurture their talents. Kroc actively mentored and trained his potential successors. He shared his knowledge, insights and experiences and encouraged people to learn from both successes and failures. As Kroc got older, he knew it was time to transition leadership. In 1974, he appointed Fred Turner as CEO. Kroc continued to serve as the business's senior chairman and later as an advisor, ensuring a smooth transition of leadership without abrupt changes. In my view, Kroc had not just worked out his succession plan but he had also worked on a backup plan as well as other ways to achieve the outcomes he wanted by building a trusted team.

- **Yahoo.** Yahoo, once the internet leader, faced a series of leadership changes and failed succession attempts during a period of decline in the early 2000s. According to an article by Patricia Lenkov published on LinkedIn in 2016, 'Lessons on succession planning from Yahoo's revolving door of CEOs', Yahoo struggled with CEO turnover during a critical phase of technological change in the digital industry. These leadership transitions contributed to instability and impacted the business's competitiveness.

- **Infosys.** Infosys, an Indian multinational IT business, has taken an approach to succession planning that emphasises leadership development and nurturing the internal talent pipeline by grooming its own leaders from within. This ensures potential successors and backups in place. Infosys also has a policy of avoiding non-family members assuming senior leadership positions. Infosys's preference for internal candidates shows a deep trust in the capabilities and potential of its own people. This fosters loyalty and motivation among people. However, it also raises questions about diversity and inclusion in leadership. Relying solely on internal talent pools limits the diversity of perspectives and experiences at the top levels of the business.

Small to medium-sized businesses with succession planning in mind

The following real-life and lived-in examples come from some of the people I've had the privilege to work with and who have been willing to share their experiences of succession planning for the future. Here are just some of their insights.

- **Jane Save, The Save Group:** 'We have a yearly plan to move them up the ladder. We also have a buddy system, where juniors work under seniors to learn.'

- **Wes Blundy, Curvy:** 'We keep giving our future stars more and more responsibility to create more capability.'

- **Scott Orpin, MEGT:** 'I do it in categories of ready now, ready in 1–3 years and ready in 3–5 years.'

- **Ali Koschel, Hunter New England and Central Coast Primary Health Network (HNECC PHN):** 'Look for potential in people, offer support and opportunities for them to step up.'

- **Sam Mathers, Fitter Futures:** 'I am mentoring experienced people who want equity in the business one day.'

- **Nicole Bryant, The Macro Group:** 'We employ external coaches to help us with the development of future leaders.'

- **Kate Save, Be Fit Food:** 'I encourage the people to look outside their own departments for talent.'

Actions

To create the right talent within your business, I recommend you focus on three key actions:

- **Leveraging the Skill Will Matrix to pinpoint people with potential.** This tool helps identify those with both the skill and eagerness to take on new challenges, providing a clear roadmap for talent development.

- **Tailoring developmental programs for your standout performers.** By offering targeted initiatives such as skill-building workshops, mentorship opportunities and stretch assignments, you can fuel their growth and encourage them towards leadership roles.

- **Creating a culture of knowledge sharing to facilitate the transfer of expertise.** Implement initiatives like mentorship programs and cross-functional projects to encourage experienced people to pass on their knowledge to emerging talent pool of people.

These three actions will help to set you up for succession planning success!

#1. Use the Skill Will Matrix to identify high-potential talent

One of the main reasons for succession planning is to identify and nurture high-potential talent within the business.

Start by identifying people who demonstrate not only the required skills and competencies but also the desire and the potential to take on leadership roles in the future. You can identify such people using tools including performance evaluations, feedback from managers and talent assessments.

As business leaders and owners, you want to create a talent pool of people who have been earmarked for potential leadership positions. This pool can serve as a source for future leaders and allows for targeted approaches.

The Skill Will Matrix, developed by Paul Hersey and leadership expert Ken Blanchard in the 1990s, has been a particularly valuable model in my experience. This framework categorises people based on their skill level and willingness to perform tasks. By looking at both competence and motivation, the Skill Will Matrix offers insights into how to tailor leadership approaches, allocate responsibilities and provide support to team members.

Business leaders and owners can use the Skill Will Matrix to assess their people's performance based on their skill and their will:

1. **Skill:** This refers to how good people are at a specific task or how effective they are in their role. It is based on their level of expertise and the knowledge required to do the role.

2. **Will:** This refers to how motivated people are to complete a task or perform their role well.

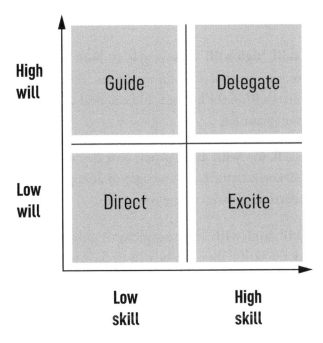

The Skill Will Matrix

It's often easier to assess someone's skill versus their will, as skill can be measured and evaluated objectively. In the workplace, some skills come naturally, while others are honed over time. Will, on the other hand, can be built up or torn down depending on a person's personal and professional goals, their workplace culture, and the support system they have in place.

The Skill Will Matrix offers flexibility and can be implemented in many ways, such as when your people return to work after a period of leave or when you're onboarding new team members, but for this action, we want to use it as an assessment tool for succession planning. The matrix can help you work out who is capable of stepping up and moving 'up the ladder'.

This framework says that people fall into one of two categories:

- Those that have the skills but lack the drive (will) to excel.

- Those that show their motivation (will) to perform but lack the skills.

In the Skill Will Matrix:

- **High skill, high will:** These people are both highly motivated and have the essential skills for their roles. They are the top performers within the business and are ideal candidates for succession planning.

- **High skill, low will:** These people have the necessary skills but lack motivation. They show signs of disengagement or dissatisfaction in their current role.

- **Low skill, high will:** These people are highly motivated but lack the skills. They may be new to their roles or require additional training.

- **Low skill, low will:** These people lack both the necessary skills and motivation to perform. They are considered challenging to work with.

The Skill Will Matrix can help you identify people with high will and high skill (your 'star' people) who may be ready for more challenging roles. From a business leader and owner perspective, you may also be looking for someone who can be part of your succession planning strategy.

#2. Create a targeted developmental program for your 'star' people

Succession planning is not just about ensuring a smooth transition of leadership but also about identifying skills gaps and providing a roadmap for people to have the necessary competencies. This investment in training and development not only prepares people for future roles but also improves their current performance.

Once you identify high will and high skill people (your stars) using the Skill Will Matrix, it's essential to provide them with the development and training opportunities they need to thrive. This can include leadership training programs, mentoring, coaching and exposure to cross-functional roles.

Encourage people to set individual development plans and career goals. Support them in acquiring the skills and experiences they need to progress within the business.

Consider offering stretch assignments or special projects to your star people to help them gain valuable leadership experience.

In my own businesses, I have implemented the following strategies to help me develop my high-performing stars:

- Holding leadership development workshops that cover essential leadership skills, such as communication, decision-making, conflict resolution and strategic thinking, then creating a series of workshops that focus on specific leadership competencies such as effective communication techniques for leaders.

- Pairing people earmarked for succession with experienced mentors who can provide guidance, share insights and offer constructive feedback. Each successor has a mentor who is a current leader in the business. The mentor provides regular one-on-one sessions and helps the successor set and achieve their career goals.

- Exposing potential successors to various roles and departments within the business to broaden their perspective and experience. A rotation program can be helpful here, which enables successors to spend a designated time working in different departments, such as marketing, finance and operations.

- Providing financial support or time off for further education, such as pursuing an advanced degree or certifications relevant to their leadership roles. Offering time off to study and financial assistance can support those who want to do higher-level industry-specific certifications but may not be able to justify the time or expense.

- Encouraging successors to build a professional network and engage in industry-related activities to stay informed about current trends and best practices. You might ask potential successors to attend and present at conferences, where they can network and learn from industry leaders.

You can also get feedback from peers, people that report to you and managers to help successors understand their strengths and areas for improvement by having a 360-degree feedback process, where anonymous feedback is collected from colleagues, team members and senior leaders. This feedback is used to create coaching and career plans.

#3. Facilitate knowledge transfer

Ineffective knowledge transfer can jeopardise actions #1 and #2 when it comes to succession planning.

Creating a knowledge transfer process for successors in your business is essential to ensure the effective transition of leadership and to preserve critical knowledge.

First, you need to determine who within the business possesses critical knowledge and expertise that needs to be transferred. These knowledge-holders are typically experienced people and long-time leaders.

Encourage knowledge-holders to document their insights, best practices, processes and any other relevant information. This documentation can include written manuals, process documents or even video recordings.

Pair successors with knowledge-holders for a period of mentorship and shadowing (part of the targeted plan in Action #2). This hands-on experience allows successors to learn directly from experienced people.

Schedule regular meetings between knowledge-holders and successors to facilitate open discussions and Q&A sessions. This provides an opportunity for sharing insights and addressing specific questions.

Encourage cross-training among high-potential people, which involves sharing responsibilities or having people temporarily take on each other's roles to gain first-hand experience in different areas of the business.

Establish systems for organising documented knowledge. This can include intranet databases, shared drives or knowledge-management software.

Recognise the efforts of knowledge holders and successors in the knowledge transfer process. Acknowledging their contributions encourages commitment to the process.

Regularly review and update the succession plan to adapt to changing business needs and to assess the readiness of potential successors. Be prepared to make adjustments as necessary.

Identifying the real stars

Imagine you run a business where certain people are complaining that they can't meet their sales targets because their colleagues (who are in a shopping centre) have more clients ready to buy in a better retail space. They are complaining because they want the same opportunity to make more sales and be incentivised by those opportunities.

(continued)

You decide to swap the two teams so you can see who is the real sales star. Guess what? The high-performing star sellers perform exceptionally well even when they are in the low-volume retail space. And the ones that were complaining? They still don't perform well, even when they are transferred to the high-volume retail space. When you have people that are the right successors, they do not blame their environment. They get on with it and make it happen!

Case study: The Tata Group

The Tata Group is one of India's largest and oldest conglomerates, dating back to the 19th century. The group has diverse business interests, including steel, automobiles, information technology and more.

As India's *The Economic Times* observed back in 2011, the Tata Group has a long-standing tradition of effective succession planning, where leadership transitions are planned to ensure transfer of power.

The focus is on identifying and supporting internal talent to step into leadership roles.

The Tata Group has a talent identification process in place. High will and high skill people are identified early in their careers and provided with training and mentorship to prepare them for leadership roles.

Successors are trained with role-specific training. For instance, people earmarked to lead Tata's businesses receive in-depth training in those sectors, gaining a deep understanding of the businesses they will eventually lead.

The group focuses on mentoring. Successors often work closely with current leaders, learning from their experience and gaining insight into the business's culture and values.

The Tata Group involves the board of directors in succession planning decisions. The board plays an active role in assessing and approving leadership transitions, ensuring transparency and good governance.

The Tata Group's culture and core values, which include integrity and commitment to social responsibility, are passed on to successors to ensure the preservation of the business's identity.

Case study: Bega Cheese

An Australian example of a small to medium-sized business that has excelled in succession planning is Bega Cheese Limited. Bega Cheese, originally founded in 1899 as a dairy cooperative in the town of Bega in New South Wales, has grown to become one of Australia's leading dairy and food companies.

Bega Cheese's success story in succession planning is known for its approach to leadership transition. The business experienced a significant turning point in 2008 when Barry Irvin assumed the role of Executive Chairman. Irvin, who had been with Bega Cheese for over three decades, knew the importance of cultivating leaders from within to sustain the business's growth and navigate the challenges of the dairy industry. (Sally Patten's 2022 interview with Barry Irvin in the *Australian Financial Review* — 'This executive's life changed with an autism diagnosis' — provides an insight into how he developed this deeper understanding of the importance of cultivating leaders.)

In 2011, Irvin initiated a strategic move by appointing Aidan Coleman as CEO. Coleman had a background in law and finance and had been with Bega Cheese for several years, demonstrating a deep understanding of the business's operations and values. This decision reflected Bega Cheese's commitment to succession planning by selecting a leader who not only had the necessary skills but also had a strong connection to the business.

The success of Bega Cheese's succession planning was further emphasised in 2017 when Paul van Heerwaarden, who had been with the business for 27 years, succeeded Aidan Coleman as CEO. Van Heerwaarden had held various positions within the business, including Group CFO, and his appointment represented a seamless transition driven by careful planning and internal talent development.

One key part of Bega Cheese's approach to succession planning was the focus on a talent development program. The business invested in training and mentorship initiatives, allowing people to gain exposure to different parts of the business.

This not only identified high-potential individuals but also equipped them with the skills necessary for leadership roles.

Bega Cheese's commitment to creating leaders from within has contributed to its success in a highly competitive industry.

Under the leadership of Paul van Heerwaarden, the business has undertaken strategic acquisitions, including the iconic Vegemite brand in 2017, expanding its product portfolio and market presence.

Reflections

Before diving into the questions that follow, ensure you have a journal and a pen within reach to capture your thoughts. Refer to Chapter 1 if you need a reminder on how to create the ideal setting for these reflections about your business. Consider the questions and journal your answers. Remember, you may also like to ask the people in your business to reflect on the same questions.

The questions are broken down into several sections. Separating the questions into distinct areas allows for a more structured and focused approach to addressing each aspect of developing your succession plan. By breaking down the discussion into specific topics, we can go deeper into each area, explore relevant questions, and develop actionable insights and strategies. This approach facilitates a more detailed way of looking at important aspects. Additionally, the discussion into separate sections helps maintain clarity and coherence, making it easier for you to track progress and identify areas for further exploration or improvement.

Initiating the succession planning discussion:

- Have you got a succession plan in place?

- Do you have a Plan A, B, and C?

- If not, which level do you think needs immediate attention?

Identifying key people:

- Can you put your key people into the Skill Will Matrix?

- Who do you think you should 'earmark' as a successor?

- Who do you foresee as someone you may need to let go in the short to medium term?

Establishing developmental plans:

- What plans do you need in place for the growth of your successors?

- Can you create a knowledge transfer process for critical roles?

- What specific leadership qualities are needed for your business?

- What coaching programs can you establish to support the growth of emerging leaders?

- What challenges do you foresee in the development of potential successors?

Identifying potential leaders:

- Which skills and competencies highlight potential leaders within your business?

- Who among your potential successors has demonstrated a commitment to continuous learning?

- Can you identify projects that showcased the leadership potential of your Plan B?

Encouraging future leaders:

- What can you do to encourage the identification and development of future leaders?

- What training can you explore to broaden the skills of potential successors?

Handling unexpected changes:

- What can you do if identified successors face unexpected challenges or changes?

- How can you prepare for unexpected shifts in leadership roles?

Summary

Succession planning is a powerful tool for retaining key people in your business. It provides clear paths for career advancement, showcasing a commitment to people development and growth. When people see a future for themselves within the business, they are more likely to stay, which fosters engagement, commitment and alignment with the business's goals.

As a business leader and owner, the lack of a well thought out succession plan can lead to stress, sleepless nights and challenges when it comes to replacing key people. Having Plans A, B and C in place is not only good practice but crucial for business continuity and peace of mind.

The Plan A, B and C strategy involves having not just one succession plan but multiple plans, ensuring that if one key person leaves, there's a person who is well prepared and ready to step in. It's about elevating the people you've already earmarked through the positions on their career trajectory, ensuring a smooth transition and avoiding rushed decisions.

While it may seem simplistic to talk about Plans A, B and C, the focus here is on the clarity of having a comprehensive succession plan. By showing people that they are valued and have a clear career path within the business, succession planning can increase people's loyalty and commitment to the business. Implementing this strategy requires extra time, energy and investment, but it alleviates the worries associated with unexpected leadership changes.

The extra costs involved in this strategy are investments in developing competencies, capabilities and, most importantly, the confidence of potential successors. Though there might not be an exact timeline for when a person might leave, a proactive approach to succession planning significantly reduces business risks.

PART II
RETAINING THE RIGHT PEOPLE

CHAPTER 4
BELIEVE IN PEOPLE

Fostering friendships and delivering feedback

Every person needs others to believe in them. Your people need that. Especially from you, as the business leader and owner. When you don't believe in your people, they become disengaged and unproductive, and then they leave.

When you believe in your people, you engage them at a deeper level — which helps you retain people.

In this chapter, I will discuss two key actions:

- fostering friendships at work

- implementing an effective approach to giving and receiving feedback.

Confidence is a key element for people to achieve success. When you believe in your people, you provide a foundation from which they can build their confidence. This belief acts as a support system, helping people feel valued and that they are capable.

When you believe in your people, you empower them to take on challenging tasks and responsibilities. It also is a recognition of your people's efforts and achievements.

When people are confident, they are more courageous when making decisions and collaborating in the workplace. This is why you want to create more self-belief in your people. It's also the right thing to do!

As a business leader and owner, when you acknowledge your people's achievements, you are going to create a positive work environment. When you praise your people for their successes, they are more likely to repeat those behaviours. As the saying goes, 'What you appreciate, appreciates!'

Recognising your people and their work helps build trust and rapport between you and your people. When you focus on rewarding great work, you create a positive culture where the focus is on people doing the right thing (rather than putting people in the spotlight for making a mistake, which leaves people feeling exposed or isolated).

Samuel's belief in people

Once upon a time, in a small village there lived a wise old farmer named Samuel. Samuel was known far and wide for his harvests and thriving fields. People commented at his crops and the abundance of his livestock. However, what set Samuel apart from others was not just his farming abilities but also his belief in people.

One morning, as the villagers gathered to sow their crops, Samuel stood before them and said, 'I have great faith in each of you. I believe in your potential, your dedication and your abilities. Together, we can accomplish remarkable things. I'm going to give you a unique opportunity this year. Each of you can choose a piece of my land to cultivate and I will provide you with the seeds and guidance you need. I trust that, with your hard work and commitment, our village will prosper ever more.'

The villagers were taken aback by Samuel's offer. No-one had ever trusted them to this extent. They hesitated but accepted his challenge. They chose plots of land, planted the seeds and took care of their crops with a new sense of purpose.

Throughout the growing season, Samuel continued to support and encourage them. He shared his knowledge, offered experience and celebrated their progress. He believed in their abilities and knew that they could excel.

As the harvest season approached, the village had transformed. The fields now had thriving crops. The villagers couldn't believe their eyes. Their hard work and Samuel's belief had yielded an amazing harvest.

In the end, the village not only had an abundant supply of food but also a sense of self-worth. They had discovered their potential and capabilities, thanks to Samuel's belief in their abilities. They had created a workplace, or in this case, a community, filled with trust, collaboration and a shared sense of purpose.

The parable of Samuel and his village shows the importance of believing in your people: giving them a piece of their own land within your business and allowing them to grow that area of the business, with you providing coaching and mentoring along the way.

When you trust and invest in the potential of those you work with, you foster an environment where creativity, collaboration and dedication can flourish. Just as Samuel's belief in the villagers led to a harvest, your belief in your people can lead to a workplace filled with achievement and growth for you, your people and your business.

Nelson Mandela and the impact of his beliefs

Nelson Mandela is globally known for his role in ending apartheid and becoming the first Black president of South Africa. His leadership style and his belief in the potential of the people he led was truly remarkable. He is one of my personal heroes.

Nelson Mandela was imprisoned for 27 years for his involvement in anti-apartheid activities. During his incarceration, he continued to advocate for justice and equality. What made Mandela's leadership exceptional was his ability to unite a deeply divided nation upon his release from prison.

He could have easily sought revenge or retribution, given the decades of injustice and oppression he had endured — but he chose a different path.

Mandela believed in the potential of all South Africans, regardless of their race, and he sought to create harmony. He promoted reconciliation, forgiveness and the idea of a 'Rainbow Nation', where people of all backgrounds could live together in peace and equality. He demonstrated patience, empathy and resilience, often putting the needs of his country and its people above his personal desires.

Under his leadership, South Africa transitioned from apartheid to become a democratic nation and Mandela became a symbol of hope, unity and human potential. His belief in South African people to overcome their divisions and build a better future created extraordinary results.

Mandela's legacy as a leader who believed in and empowered his people continues to inspire leaders worldwide to place their trust in the potential of those they lead and to work towards a more just and inclusive society.

Examples of the importance of believing in people

Nelson Mandela's belief in his people resonates with business due to his inclusive leadership, empowerment, social responsibility, resilience and visionary thinking. Mandela's principles offer valuable lessons for creating ethical, sustainable and impactful businesses that focus on the wellbeing of the business and its people.

Many businesses conduct regular people engagement surveys to assess their business's satisfaction and identify areas of improvement. These surveys often include questions related to leaving intentions and reasons. Some businesses conduct 'pulse surveys' which can be as short as one to two minutes to get a 'pulse' on how their people are travelling.

Websites such as LinkedIn often publish business reports that provide an insight into job trends and employee satisfaction. Glassdoor is a platform where people can anonymously review their business leaders and owner. Analysing people's reviews can reveal common issues and reasons for leaving a business. Gallup's annual 'State of the Global Workplace' report provides valuable insights into people engagement and the factors that influence it. Understanding why people may feel undervalued could make all the difference to a business's bottom line.

Businesses often calculate the cost of people leaving to understand its financial implications. These calculations consider factors such as recruitment costs, training expenses and lost productivity.

Some businesses even use predictive analytics to forecast which people are at the highest risk of leaving. These models consider historical leaving data and a range of variables to identify potential flight risks.

Here are a couple of real-world business examples of businesses who seem to believe in their people:

- **HubSpot**, a marketing software business, is known for its people feedback. It has implemented a program where people can nominate their colleagues for recognition.

- **Facebook**, now Meta Platforms, Inc., conducts 'Q&A with Mark' sessions where people can ask questions and provide feedback directly to the CEO, Mark Zuckerberg.

Small to medium-sized businesses and how they nurture their people

The following real-life and lived examples come from some of the people I've had the privilege to work with and who have been willing to share how they support their people. Perhaps these insights can guide you too.

- **Jane Save, The Save Group:** 'We do a daily huddle, weekly meeting, monthly meeting, quarterly and annual strategy meetings off-site, annual goal setting and performance reviews, people analyser to core values.'

- **Wes Blundy, Curvy:** 'We use a fabulous tool called office vibe which surveys everyone weekly with rotating questions. You also do quarterly conversations which is a performance review with their manager.'

- **Scott Orpin, MEGT:** 'Regular and consistent time with them — weekly, fortnightly or monthly provide context, context, context or meaning for the work they are doing.'

- **Annika Launay, PDPR Marketing + Creative:** 'You can't underestimate the power of simply asking questions and listening to hear.'

- **Kate Winter, Champion Web:** 'Having a one-to-one session with each individual. Having individual and people goals.'

- **Liberte Guthrie, Liberte Property & Crossroad Developments:** 'KPI weekly check-in calls, daily touch base and annual reviews.'

- **Angus Nicol, Black Market Coffee:** 'Face to face, regular streams of WhatsApp messages, people parties.'

- **Ali Koschel, Hunter New England and Central Coast Primary Health Network (HNECC PHN):** 'Door open, stand transparent with them. Regular monthly catch-up, more often if required.'

- **Nancy Youssef, Classic Mentoring:** 'We run EOS management system which is great for people engagement and development.'

- **Sam Mathers, Fitter Futures:** 'We have quarterly reviews with each [member] to check in.'

Actions

There are many actions you can take when it comes to retaining people in your business — and believing in people comes top of the list for me. The two actions I highlight here are not the complete list. Here, I want to talk about the top two actions that have helped me and my clients to retain key people and see them thrive. First, however, it is important to understand why people might decide to leave your business.

Why do people leave?

The direct relationship with their manager is one of the most common reasons people leave. People who feel disengaged or unappreciated by their managers are more likely to seek other job opportunities. Conflicts with other people or managers can make the business environment challenging for people as these conflicts lead to stress.

Money tends not to be the primary reason that people leave their jobs, which is assumed and/or often given as a reason for leaving in exit interviews. The real reason may be a lack of opportunities for career development and growth. People often seek roles that allow them to learn new skills, take on more responsibility and advance in their careers. Leaders that do not provide a clear path for progression lose key and high-performing people (the 'A' players from Chapter 2). If people don't feel that their skills align with their job role, they may seek positions where they can better use their skills.

This topic of balance has been discussed for over 20 years. What this means when it comes to people leaving is that jobs that demand excessive hours or offer little flexibility can lead to burnout and job dissatisfaction. People leave in search of positions that provide a better work-life balance. Since COVID, many people have found they want to switch to reduced hours or permanent part-time work.

Money does come into play for some people who believe they are not fairly paid for their skills and are more likely to leave and explore other opportunities, especially if they receive better offers elsewhere. In 2023, career website Indeed indicated that money has become a more pressing reason for leaving since the cost of living has been going up.

A negative or toxic business culture, with poor communication, bullying, discrimination or harassment, will drive people away. A healthy business culture, where people feel safe and valued, is key for retention.

People thrive on recognition and appreciation for their efforts. A lack of acknowledgment for their hard work and contributions can lead to people feeling disengaged and demotivated, making them more likely to leave.

Uncertainty about job security, such as frequent redundancies or restructuring, is another factor that can create anxiety, leading people to explore more stable employment options. This happened more during COVID.

As many businesses are coming back into the office environment, long commutes or business locations can be the reason that people leave their job. Many businesses are now wanting to have their people return at least three days a week. People have got used to working from home and for some people, being questioned about how they are spending their work time is off-putting, especially if they are being asked to return to the office when there is no need for them to be in the office. As a result of not negotiating or discussing the options in a collaborative way, these businesses may be losing key people.

Flexible work arrangements are no longer a nice to have, it is expected that the business allows people to have flexibility including remote work. Many businesses are still struggling with the percentage of office-based versus home workers, but working from home is here to stay. The percentage may shift. Even some of the small to large businesses I have spoken to will do 4:1 (which is four days in the office and one from home) or 3:2 (with three days being in the office).

Depending on your business, it is important that your people see that you trust them and are outcome-focused not just fixated on the number of hours people spend in the office!

Do you know why your people are leaving?

Conducting interviews and reviewing exit data is an important strategy. If you as a business leader and owner are currently not conducting exit interviews, this is the first thing you may want to consider changing.

In my experience, the ideal time to conduct an exit interview is as soon as possible after people resign. Leaving the exit interview until the day before they leave means they'll be completely disengaged and ready to move on to their new role, mentally at least.

Conduct an exit interview with you as the business leader/owner and your HR person (not with another manager that the person may report to, as their reason may very well be the manager themselves, and they are unlikely to open up in the exit interview if this is the case). Also setting up the interview as confidential is key.

Analysing the resulting interview data, you may notice common themes such as dissatisfaction with management, lack of career growth opportunities or work-life balance issues. This data needs to be discussed at your strategy planning sessions to discuss what needs to change in order to ensure higher retention of people.

#1. Foster and encourage friendships within your business

In recent years, loneliness in business has gained recognition as a significant and growing concern. Often referred to as the 'next pandemic', the impact of workplace loneliness is not only key to your people's wellbeing but also to increasing productivity in the workplace.

A study reported in 2021 in the *Harvard Business Review* highlighted that over 60 per cent of people across various industries reported feeling lonely at work. The shift towards remote work and our increased reliance on digital communication tools, especially as a result of changes since the COVID-19 pandemic, has contributed to a sense of isolation among people. The lack of face-to-face interactions and the absence of a physical workplace community have been identified as key factors making loneliness worse.

Workplace loneliness is associated with various negative outcomes, including decreased job satisfaction, lower engagement levels, and higher levels of stress and burnout. It can also hinder collaboration and teamwork, leading to a decline in overall business performance. The long-term effects of persistent loneliness at work may even contribute to attrition rates and difficulties in talent retention.

Having a friend at work is a remedy for loneliness and means that the people in your business will know they have a friend that believes in them.

Business friendships often translate into improved work outcomes and more effective collaboration. People who are friends tend to communicate better, resolve conflicts more effectively and work better together. This synergy creates a positive work environment and job satisfaction.

Having friends at work creates a sense of belonging and inclusion. The five key areas that benefit most from business friendships are:

1. **Emotional support:** Having a friend at work provides emotional support, creating a sense of belonging and camaraderie. This emotional connection helps people navigate the challenges of the workplace, reducing feelings of isolation and loneliness.

2. **Increased job satisfaction:** Friendships at work contribute to increased job satisfaction. When people feel a sense of connection with their colleagues, they are more likely to enjoy their work environment, leading to greater overall job satisfaction.

3. **Collaboration and teamwork:** Friendships foster collaboration and teamwork. When people have positive relationships with their co-workers, they are more inclined to share ideas, communicate effectively, and collaborate on projects. This, in turn, enhances team dynamics and productivity.

4. **Stress reduction:** Workplace friendships serve as a buffer against stress. Having someone to share challenges with, seek advice from, or simply vent to can significantly reduce stress levels, promoting better mental health.

5. **Improved job performance:** A 2018 article published in the *Personality and Social Psychology Bulletin* ('Friends with performance benefits: a meta-analysis on the relationship between friendship and group performance') suggests that having friends at work is positively correlated with job performance. The social support gained from these relationships contributes to increased motivation and a sense of commitment to the business.

Addressing workplace loneliness is essential for cultivating a positive and productive work environment. Encouraging the development of friendships at work is not just a matter of creating a pleasant atmosphere but a strategic approach to enhancing your people's wellbeing and business success.

As businesses navigate the challenges of remote work and changing dynamics, prioritising social connections within the workplace becomes an integral part of fostering a resilient and thriving workforce.

Business is where people spend a large portion of their lives. Forming connections and friendships can be a key factor in people retention. And having that someone at work that is a confidant and believes in you can make all the difference to your work.

How can you encourage friendships at work as a business leader or owner?

A good place to start is to create spaces within the business that encourage collaboration and informal interactions. For example, Google's offices are renowned for their innovative workspace designs, including open lounges, game rooms and communal eating areas.

I have implemented these spaces both in business and at home. In the workplace, I place lounges near the coffee machine where people can interact while getting a cup of tea or coffee.

Organising regular people-building (team-building) activities helps people bond and build friendships. Zappos, the online shoe and clothing retailer, is known for its fun and quirky people-building events, such as scavenger hunts and themed parties.

When I have organised such events, it is important to ensure all activities are inclusive. For example, hiking up a hill or doing water sports may not work for every person in your team.

Inclusive social events cater to diverse interests. Airbnb, for instance, has previously held People Resource Group events where people with similar interests or backgrounds could connect outside of work.

I used to regularly organise a joint team lunch where everyone would bring a dish that was easy for them to prepare or buy. As we had a diverse group of people, the lunches were delicious and everyone bonded over the amazing food! People would be active on the WhatsApp chat about what they were bringing, sharing recipes and feeling more grateful for the culture they worked in.

Another way to encourage professional friendships is to assign people to cross-functional projects or task forces. This allows people from different departments to collaborate and form friendships.

In one of my businesses, I implemented a cross-functional collaboration approach where the most junior team member met quarterly with their manager to discuss strategies and operational improvements. This initiative sparked an increase in projects to improve business operations. It empowered people by giving them a different perspective.

Here are a few other ways you can foster workplace friendships within your business's culture.

ENCOURAGING COMMUNITY

There is a growing trend that people are giving up their breaks and sitting at their desks for longer. COVID exacerbated that problem. Despite being able to work from home, people are going from one meeting to another without any breaks in between.

In recent years, it has been said that 'sitting is the new smoking'. So, in your office environment, what better way to highlight the need to move away from your desk than by encouraging people to meet for a walk or a stretch, to have a walking meeting, or to share lunch in a communal area?

One day a week my husband and I work together from home. We ensure that for lunch, we meet for about 20 minutes in the kitchen to prepare our food together and then we sit outside in the sun. And we are not alone. Businesses like Pixar have designed their campuses with communal dining areas, where people are encouraged to share meals and engage in informal conversations.

REFERRING FOR MUTUAL REWARD

To bring in great people, I recommend you introduce a referral system, which may include a reward for a successful referrer. In my business, if a person who already works for us refers someone and they are a successful hire, we give them $500 (much cheaper than a recruiter), and on the new recruit's one-year anniversary, we give the referrer another $500. Most people do not want to recommend people to join the business who are a dickhead — for their reputation's sake if nothing else.

This system also fosters friendships at work because it encourages people to think about growing the team and recommending great people to work with. We call this the 'no dickhead' policy!

CELEBRATING PERSONAL MILESTONES AND ACHIEVEMENTS

Taking note of and celebrating people's personal milestones and achievements is a sure-fire way to connect the people in your team. You might want to recognise birthdays or anniversaries or the birth of a child, or even honour a shared anniversary, such as for the workplace or office location — like a work birthday.

In one of my earlier businesses, each employee was able to take their birthday off fully paid. The engagement that this created in my business was beyond what words could explain. People felt seen. They had a day where they could celebrate themselves, catch up with family or friends or go and have a walk or a massage. I received so many emails from people who appreciated the gesture. And one day of labour costs was a minimal cost for the engagement it created. In interviews, our manager would proudly speak about this feature as part of the culture in our business.

Another way to recognise people is to celebrate their professional achievements. Adobe, for example, hosts recognition events, where people are celebrated for their contributions.

CREATING AN OPEN, TRANSPARENT CULTURE

Open and transparent communication within the business encourages people to connect on a personal level. If, as a business leader or owner, you are going through some personal challenges, try sharing them with your business leaders and managers. It helps them understand why it may appear that you are not on your 'A game'. It also creates empathy for you. You don't have to share the details (for example, if you are going through a divorce) but just the headline will help them understand.

As we were navigating through COVID, I was really transparent with my people that there were some financial struggles ahead as we did not know what our landlords were going to do regarding rent and it was unclear at first if there was going to be any government support. By communicating transparently with my people, they had more empathy with the business's struggles. I kept my people updated daily so they always knew the latest developments.

My website is set up as askshivani.com for that reason!

HubSpot, a marketing software business, emphasises open communication through regular business-wide updates and 'Ask Me Anything' sessions with executives.

#2. The importance of feedback, and knowing how to deliver it

If one of the most common reasons for people to leave their jobs is due to their direct relationship with their manager, this should be ringing alarm bells, sending goosebumps up your arms, or causing some kind of major emotional reaction if you're a business leader or owner. It does alarm me. Is it alarming to you?

A manager is a person your people will spend a lot of time and energy thinking about. People work closely with their managers — a manager is the person who lets your people know that their work has been noticed, and a manager tells people when they are doing a good job. A manager is also the person who lets your people know what they may need to change if they want to excel in their roles.

The saying, 'No news is good news' is the 'old' way of thinking about the employee-manager relationship, in my view.

The new way of thinking is for every person in a successful business to have a great relationship with their manager.

Businesses can significantly outperform financially when they invest in their people. In 2021, the Society for Human Resource Management (SHRM) published an article indicating that businesses that prioritise their people can be one to three times more likely to surpass their peers financially. This means that when a business takes care of its people — through good management practices, career development opportunities, competitive compensation and fostering a positive work environment—it creates a motivated team. A motivated team is more productive, innovative and committed, which directly contributes to better financial results.

People are the lifeblood of any business, and by recognising their value and investing in their wellbeing and professional growth, businesses don't just grow in human capital but also see tangible gains in their financial outcomes. This strategy turns people satisfaction into a competitive advantage that drives the company's success.

Regular feedback from a manager allows people to identify areas for improvement and growth. Constructive feedback from a manager provides your people with valuable insights into their performance, helping them to make adjustments to their actions and behaviours and develop their skills.

Using the 4:1 ratio of feedback

One day, in a workshop, I was introduced to the concept of the 4:1 feedback ratio as a key principle for enhancing both leadership effectiveness and personal development. This ratio looks at the importance of providing four positive pieces of feedback for every piece of constructive feedback (which may seem more negative).

The 4:1 ratio of feedback centres on the idea that positive feedback should far exceed negative feedback. In other words, you want to catch your people doing something right (rather than wrong).

Just like managing a bank account, it's crucial to understand the balance between giving and taking when it comes to feedback with your team. I often explain to managers the concept of the 4:1 ratio, which works a lot like maintaining a healthy bank balance. Before you can make a withdrawal, you need to ensure you've made enough deposits. In the context of managing people, every bit of positive feedback or praise is like a deposit, and every piece of constructive criticism is like a withdrawal.

You should aim to give your team at least four positive reinforcements for every one piece of criticism. If you keep taking — that is, delivering critiques to your people without recognising their hard work and successes — you'll end up with an overdrawn account. This leads to a team that feels undervalued and unmotivated. Remember, if you haven't built up a reservoir of goodwill through regular and sincere positive feedback, you shouldn't be surprised if your attempts to 'withdraw' with critiques lead to negative balances in engagement and morale. Keep the 'account' of each team member healthy with a steady stream of positive feedback so that when you need to offer guidance or correction, it doesn't bankrupt their trust and confidence.

How can they be engaged, if they feel that everything they do (according to their manager) suggests they're perpetually 'stuffing up' or getting things wrong?

After a while, many people switch off when they realise their manager is coming to see them to give them feedback. They feel there will be nothing positive about the encounter before it has even happened.

Getting feedback from the business leader or owner regularly is really important as well. It's like having a coach who's always helping you play better. When your manager tells you what you're doing well and what you can improve on often, it helps you stay on top of your game. You feel more a part of the team, and you're less likely to think about leaving your job because you know where you stand and how you can grow. It's that simple — when bosses talk to their team and give them pointers right when they need them, everyone does better.

Imagine if one of your people is making the same mistake in the business for a period of 12 months. For example, it may be a mistake in a proposal to a client that if not corrected, means that every proposal will carry the same mistake. If the mistake costs the business an extra $150 each time and the individual sends out 100 proposals during those 12 months, the minimum loss to the business is $15 000 for one person for one mistake! If left uncorrected, habits may also become fixed and be harder to break.

I have two children who are both teenagers. If I were to give them feedback in 12 months' time for something they're doing now, they would look at me as if I have lost my mind. For those of you with teenagers, you know the look I'm talking about!

Providing feedback as it happens is the best way to encourage, inspire and motivate the person you are trying to support.

Creating a feedback culture

Managers need to lead by example. They need to model the behaviours that they want to see. They need to actively seek feedback and be open to receiving it as much as they are willing to give it.

Managers need to be trained in giving and receiving feedback; equally, they need to train (or provide training for) their people to ensure they are also comfortable with giving and receiving feedback.

I'll be honest: the first time I was sent to feedback training in a corporate role, I thought it was crazy. It seemed so basic to me, and I was surprised that we were wasting money on this type of training.

After the training, however, I recognised that I had learned so much about the feedback process, from the importance of eye contact and body language through to the actual words used.

You need to create a culture in which your people understand how to give feedback and how to receive it if you want to create engagement. This can include workshops on communication skills, active listening and constructive feedback.

One of the parts of the training that really helped me involved how to create a safe space for people to give and receive feedback. Giving or receiving feedback needs to be thought through and planned (even if the session itself only lasts for a couple of minutes). You want to ensure feedback is exchanged in a safe space that allows honest, respectful and non-judgemental communication.

Confession time: I will put my hand up and say that non-judgemental communication is difficult for me and the same is true for the managers I have trained. It is so easy to form opinions and pass judgement on other people, and moving away from that bias is essential for a mutually respectful feedback process.

It is also essential that your managers understand that the skill of giving and receiving feedback is not a 'nice to have' but a must-have. There should be an expectation that feedback will be given properly and is valued in the business. It can be discussed in the interview process and built into the personal and professional development part of the employee's annually reviewed career plan.

A 2015 Gallup study found that people who receive regular feedback from their managers are almost three times more likely to be engaged in their work, resulting in lower leaving rates and increased people retention.

Is giving and receiving feedback part of your current culture? If so, well done you!

If not, how can you incorporate feedback into your business's culture?

Providing coaching and mentoring for your people

Implementing coaching and mentoring programs where people can share experiences and grow as a result is essential. When someone has been an internal mentor for a period of time, then that friendship often continues to grow beyond the initial time frame. This can be used for both experienced people and newcomers. As an example, the tech company Cisco Systems offers a mentorship program that pairs seasoned people with newcomers, helping them navigate their roles and develop lasting professional relationships.

I am a member of EO (Entrepreneurs' Organization), which is a not for profit with over 18 000 members across 226 chapters in 77 countries.

It has a MY EO group for special interests. When you join as a member, you can join an existing area that suits your interest like Under 35, women, yachts, HR businesses etc. There are literally hundreds of interest groups. And if you don't happen to find one that suits your interests, you can start one and invite others to join.

I am going to get into the importance of coaching in the business in Chapter 7 and how to implement this in your business.

Case study: Adobe

A business that has created a great feedback culture to engage people and reduce turnover is Adobe, a global software business. Adobe implemented a feedback and performance management system that led to positive outcomes for both people and the business.

Adobe, like many businesses, used to conduct an annual performance review where managers provided feedback and evaluated their people's performance. This system was not producing the results it needed and was leading to disengagement.

In 2012, Adobe decided to discard the traditional annual performance reviews and replace them with a system known as 'Check-in'. The Check-in system had regular, ongoing conversations and feedback between people and their managers. These meetings focused on discussing goals, performance, career development, and any concerns or feedback.

The focus was on immediate, positive and constructive feedback. This encouraged open and honest communication between people and managers.

The Check-in system had several positive outcomes for Adobe. People reported feeling more engaged and connected to their work and their managers, Adobe experienced a significant reduction in staff turnover, people were more satisfied at their work and the continuous feedback process helped them feel valued and appreciated.

Inspired by Adobe, almost all the meetings I run with people in management start with a 30-second check-in — and it is a real check-in, not just an opportunity for your people to impress you as the business leader or owner. It is a great strategy to implement.

Reflections

Before diving into the questions that follow, ensure you have a journal and a pen within reach to capture your thoughts. Refer to Chapter 1 if you need a reminder on how to create the ideal setting for these reflections about your business. Consider the questions and journal your answers. Remember, you may also like to ask the people in your business to reflect on the same questions.

The questions are broken down into several sections. Separating the questions into distinct areas allows for a more structured and focused approach to addressing each aspect of fostering friendships and providing feedback at work. By breaking down the discussion into specific topics, we can go deeper into each area, explore relevant questions, and develop actionable insights and strategies. This approach facilitates a more detailed way of looking at important aspects. Additionally, the discussion into separate sections helps maintain clarity and coherence, making it easier for you to track progress and identify areas for further exploration or improvement.

Understanding why people are leaving:

- Do you know why your good people are leaving? List down the top three reasons.

- How are you measuring this? For example, exit interviews.

- Are there any policies you need to change?

Fostering friendships at work:

- How do you foster an environment for people to have friends at work?

- What other team-building activities and social events do you have to encourage positive interactions among your people?

- Would you consider a buddy system for new people starting in your business?

Introducing a referral system and giving people feedback:

- Do you have a referral system for people who refer their friends? Is it working?

- Are you and your managers trained in how to give feedback?

- What can do you to enhance the referral program and provide feedback training to managers? How can people feel recognised (monetarily or otherwise) for their referrals?

Implementing effective feedback practices:

- Do you and your managers give feedback using the 4:1 ratio?

- What is one thing that can be improved to give better feedback?

- How can you train managers on effective feedback techniques?

- How can you encourage a balance of positive and constructive feedback?

Introducing retention initiatives:

- What are your top three initiatives to retain top talent within our business?

- What retention strategies, such as career development programs, flexible work arrangements and recognition programs, do you need to develop?

Making cultural contributions to belief:

- What part of your culture contributes to people believing in themselves?

- What more can be done to identify and reinforce cultural elements that empower and inspire people?

- How can you better celebrate achievements?

Providing managerial feedback training:

- What training do you need to provide to help managers give more helpful feedback?

- What other training programs for managers need to be implemented on delivering effective feedback, communication skills and people development?

Implementing recognition and reward systems:

- What recognition and reward systems would reinforce people's belief?

- How can you complement a recognition program that includes both formal and informal methods to acknowledge people's efforts and accomplishments?

Providing professional development opportunities:

- What professional development can be offered to enhance people's skills and career growth within the business?

- How can a professional development plan, including training sessions, mentorship programs and opportunities for skill enhancement, be done better?

Creating communication channels for people input:

- What communication channels can be established to ensure that people feel heard and valued within the business?

- How can you implement regular town hall meetings, suggestion boxes or anonymous feedback/surveys to encourage open communication?

Offering mentorship and coaching:

- What role can mentorship and coaching play in creating a supportive business?

- What needs to be done to establish formal mentorship programs and provide coaching opportunities to support your people's professional and personal development?

Summary

Understanding why people leave a job is essential for any business leader and owner aiming to improve retention rates. Developing effective strategies to address these concerns is essential for creating a business where people feel valued, engaged and motivated.

The primary driver is the relationship with one's manager. This shows the significance of effective leadership and the need for managers to cultivate positive connections with their people.

Money is not the leading cause of people leaving. It is due to a lack of career development opportunities, work-life balance issues or dissatisfaction with the culture. Hence, as business owners and leaders we must focus on offering clear career paths, promoting a positive work-life balance and cultivating a healthy and inclusive culture to retain top talent.

As remote work continues to redefine our workplaces, the reality of workplace loneliness cannot be ignored. Strategies such as fostering business friendships can contribute to addressing loneliness, improving job satisfaction and promoting overall wellbeing. Cultivating a culture that promotes business friendships addresses this isolation, as these relationships are key to enhancing job fulfilment and improving collaboration.

To manifest these insights into tangible retention strategies, a dual approach can be leveraged. First, nurturing business friendships through shared experiences and mentorship programs can offer solace and support, guiding employees through both professional and personal challenges. Second, nurturing a culture that values continuous, constructive feedback enables a dynamic environment where open communication is not just encouraged but expected. Embracing these parts can lead to a successful journey for a business, setting the stage for creating a workplace that doesn't just attract talent but believes in its people and, in doing so, retains them.

CHAPTER 5
SHOSHIN

Encouraging lifelong learning

Businesses are constantly being 'upgraded' as a result of change and innovation, making it important for people to adapt and learn new skills throughout their careers. As business leaders and owners, we need people that are lifelong learners — or at least willing to be.

I recently took my daughter (who is in high school) to a university open day. We attended four lectures in various careers. Each session mentioned that this generation will have six to eight careers. That is a lot of careers, and each of those careers will require a lot of *shoshin* with each transition into the next career.

Shoshin refers to a 'beginner's mind', which is a concept rooted in Zen Buddhism and can be applied to personal growth, creativity and learning. It is the idea of looking at situations and experiences with an open, curious and humble mindset, regardless of experience. It encourages you to adopt the mind of a beginner, even when you've got plenty of experience, knowledge or skills.

The term 'shoshin' consists of two Japanese characters:

- 'sho' (初) means 'beginning' or 'open'

- 'shin' (心) means 'mind' or 'heart'

Therefore, I see shoshin as the quality of having a 'beginner's mind' or 'open heart'.

Imagine if ALL the people in your business had a beginner's mind or open heart. You would be surrounded by people who did not constantly complain or make comments such as 'we've done this before and it didn't work'. 'Yes!' you might think. 'I would like more of these people in my business!'

According to the World Economic Forum's 'Future of Jobs' report, published in 2023, researchers predicted that by 2027, the top skills needed in the business world would include analytical thinking, creative thinking and AI/big data, highlighting the demand for people that are lifelong learners.

Lifelong learners often experience career growth and advancement. According to a 2016 survey from the Pew Research Center in the United States, people who engage in continuous learning are more likely to receive promotions and salary increases compared to those who do not invest in their personal and professional development.

When you approach a situation with a beginner's mind, you leave behind any preconceived ideas, biases and judgements. You're willing to see things as they are, free from the filters of your past experiences or assumptions.

I often find that it is difficult to deal with situations without judgement. But imagine if you could enter every situation without judgement and see it without any preconceptions, like a child with the wonder and curiosity of learning new things.

The shoshin mindset is exactly that. It creates a sense of curiosity and wonder, like a child exploring the world for the first time. Instead of assuming you know everything, you ask questions, seek understanding and enjoy the joy of discovery.

Having a 'shoshin' mentality also requires humility. You have to admit to yourself and others that there is always more to learn and that you don't have all the answers.

The ego can find it difficult to deal with shoshin. I think of ego the way a teacher once shared with me — as a dog on a leash. Imagine a Great Dane (or another big dog) is taking you for a walk. Then, imagine you have a Toy Cavoodle (like I do) — you're the one taking the small dog for a walk! The ego is the dog. Is the ego driving you or are you driving it?

An unhealthy ego does not want to have a beginner's mindset — it is running the show, taking you for the walk. It is in control of your mind, like the Great Dane. Shoshin encourages us to let go of our ego-driven need to prove ourselves or appear like you have all the answers.

A beginner's mind is ideal for creativity and innovation. By getting rid of assumptions, you open up new possibilities and think outside the box. When you have a beginner's mind, challenges and obstacles are seen as opportunities for growth rather than as threats.

The shoshin mentality is about living in the present moment. It encourages mindfulness and being fully engaged in the here and now.

As a business leader and owner, you want your people to have the shoshin mentality!

Hiroshi's lessons on shoshin

In a small village near the forest, there lived a wise old man named Hiroshi. Hiroshi was known throughout the village for his deep wisdom and commitment to lifelong learning.

One day, a group of young villagers approached Hiroshi, seeking his guidance. They were eager to learn the secrets of success and happiness. Hiroshi agreed to teach them, on the condition that they cultivate the shoshin mentality, approaching their lessons with open hearts and minds, as beginners.

The first lesson was about mindfulness. Hiroshi led them to a river to sit and teach. He handed each of them a small teacup and explained, 'The teacup represents your mind. It can only hold a limited amount of tea, just as your mind can hold a limited amount of knowledge. To learn, you must first empty your teacup.'

The young villagers struggled with this concept due to their ego. They thought they knew a lot and found it hard to let go of their existing beliefs and knowledge. Hiroshi demonstrated by pouring tea into their cups until they overflowed, which represented their struggle to clear their minds. The tea spilled over the sides, wasting the tea as there was no room in the cup. Then he poured tea into empty cups, and the tea sat in each cup. He said, 'To learn, one must empty the cup, embracing the shoshin mentality.' He then encouraged the villagers to drink the tea and empty their cups, which represented them emptying their minds and making room for new knowledge.

In meditation, people try and let go of attachments to thoughts and emotions, creating space for clarity, insight and learning. By emptying the cup — both literally in the tea ceremony and in meditation — one can create new knowledge and experiences.

Each lesson revolved around letting go of preconceptions and approaching new experiences with the openness of beginners. Over time, the villagers began to embrace the shoshin mentality and they felt a new-found sense of wonder about the world around them.

Shoshin was a concept I was introduced to by one of my colleagues from Entrepreneurs' Organization (EO) and who I would consider an informal mentor, Nik Bloor. I went into training for mentoring others. At this point, I had already been coaching and mentoring for over 15 years and done a variety of coaching qualifications so felt (without saying it out aloud) that I knew a thing or two about coaching and mentoring.

Even when Nik mentioned shoshin as a concept, in my head I was saying, 'Got it, now let's move to the next slide.' When I recognised my 'non-shoshin' approach, I almost laughed out loud. With a beginner's mindset, I learned a lot in that training and it has made me a better coach.

Elon Musk and shoshin

Whether you like him or not, Elon Musk is a visionary entrepreneur and founder of multiple successful businesses and is someone who in my view seems to live the shoshin mentality.

He has looked at things with a beginner's mindset and created some major shifts in what we do and how we live.

He founded SpaceX with the goal of reducing space transportation costs and moving a step towards the colonisation of Mars. Having a limited background in rocket science, he approached the aerospace industry with a beginner's mindset.

Musk learned from experts, experimented and was open about failures. SpaceX's iterative design process and Falcon 1 rocket's

(continued)

initial three failed launches showed his dedication to learning from mistakes. This approach has led to many successes, such as the Falcon 9 and Dragon spacecraft, which have advanced the future of space travel and may change the way we travel in future.

Musk also applied the shoshin mentality to the automotive industry with Tesla. He entered this sector with the goal of making electric vehicles (EVs) mainstream. Tesla faced many challenges, including technology barriers, scepticism from media and competitors, and production issues.

Musk maintained an open mind and a focus on learning. Tesla's development of the Model S, Model 3 and advancements in battery technology have made inroads into the development of more efficient EVs. Musk kept an open mind even in the face of adversity.

Musk worked with the co-founders of SolarCity, which aimed to make solar energy more accessible and affordable. SolarCity combined solar panel installation and energy storage solutions. This venture showed his willingness to have an open mind and again he wasn't an expert in the field. SolarCity was eventually acquired by Tesla.

Musk's ability to enter diverse industries and achieve extraordinary results, to approach challenges with a beginner's mindset, and continuously learn and adapt is a great example of shoshin.

Musk continues to look at the world with a fresh perspective, which is why I believe he must practice shoshin or have a similar philosophy about the world. If Musk did not practice shoshin, maybe many more obstacles, including his own experience, would have got in the way of his success.

Business leaders and owners who display a shoshin mentality

The shoshin mentality can be seen in the business world and beyond. Here are some inspirational quotes from leaders who I think display a shoshin mentality:

- **Zig Ziglar, a motivational speaker:** 'You don't have to be great to start, but you have to start to be great.'

- **Tony Robbins, life coach and author:** 'The path to success is to take massive, determined action.'

- **Jack Welch, the former CEO of General Electric:** 'An organization's' ability to learn, and translate that learning into action rapidly, is the ultimate competitive advantage.'

- **Jim Rohn, a motivational speaker:** 'Formal education will make you a living; self-education will make you a fortune.'

- **Simon Sinek, known for his work on purpose-driven leadership:** 'People don't buy what you do; they buy why you do it.'

- **Benjamin Franklin, American diplomat and one of the Founding Fathers:** 'An investment in knowledge pays the best interest.'

In the business world, shoshin seems to have empowered leaders to be bold:

- Apple's **Steve Jobs** challenged the status quo by questioning why computers and music couldn't be made portable.

- Former LEGO CEO **Jorgen Vig Knudstorp** orchestrated one of the most remarkable corporate turnarounds in history, propelling the brand from the brink of insolvency to a billion-dollar toy empire.

- **Niklas Wass**, the president of the business line Stainless Europe at Outokumpu, recognised the transformative potential of the shoshin concept in an interview with *CEO Magazine* in 2022, seeing the beginner's mind as the catalyst for innovation within the steel industry.

Small to medium-sized businesses: Encouraging lifelong learning

In my opinion, lifelong learning is important in both personal and professional realms. The evolving nature of technology, industry and global markets demands that people continually get new skills and knowledge to remain relevant. To encourage and support continuous learning within a business, it is key to create a culture that values curiosity and innovation. This can be done by providing access to educational resources, facilitating opportunities for professional development, and recognising and rewarding learning achievements. Supporting continuous education empowers people, stimulates growth, and ensures that both the people and the business and prepare for future challenges.

The following real-life and lived-in examples come from some of the people I've had the privilege to work with and who have been willing to share their experiences of encouraging lifelong learning at work. So, I asked them the question: 'In your opinion, how important is it for people to be lifelong learners and how do you encourage and support continuous learning within your business?' Here are some of their answers.

- **Kate Save, Be Fit Food:** 'One of our values is "To embrace change and grow" as small businesses need to constantly innovate and turn challenges into opportunities to succeed.'

- **Wes Blundy, Curvy:** 'I think it's essential if you want to have a great business rather than an average business.'

- **Scott Orpin, MEGT:** 'Learning inside and outside the business creates stimulation for people and teaches people to be involved.'

- **Fiona Anchal, Wholesome Bellies:** 'When you find great people members, you want to continue to grow and develop them so that they stay with the business.'

- **Annika Launay, PDPR Marketing + Creative:** 'We always encouraged our people to take on short courses and learning opportunities.'

- **Kate Winter, Champion Web:** 'Without lifelong learners there is no continuous improvement.'

- **Liberte Guthrie, Liberte Property & Crossroad Developments:** 'We cover the costs for learning courses they are interested in. Allow them to take time to study.'

- **Angus Nicol, Black Market Coffee:** 'Very important, though implementing a system for this is challenging.'

- **Ali Koschel, Hunter New England and Central Coast Primary Health Network (HNECC PHN):** 'Essential; offer support to personal learning outside of work and offer personal development.'

- **Nancy Youssef, Classic Mentoring:** 'By demonstrating my own commitment to PD (personal development).'

- **Jane Save, The Save Group:** 'Attending industry webinars on a weekly basis on employment law changes.'

- **Sam Mathers, Fitter Futures:** 'Continuous learning is one of our core values. We invest in professional development.'

- **Nicole Bryant, The Macro Group:** 'Two of our values are Progressive and Evolving, which are centred around growth and learning.'

Actions

Engaging with the world through a lens of curiosity and willingness to try, fail and try again, positively reinforces the beginner's mindset, leading to personal growth and an enhanced capacity for innovation personally and in business. These three actions are designed to help you encourage lifelong learning by creating a shoshin mentality in your business:

- **Encourage curiosity, innovation and a willingness to learn from all levels of the business.** Embracing this mindset creates an environment where fresh ideas thrive, driving continuous improvement and adaptability.

- **Embrace technology, particularly artificial intelligence (AI), as a tool for enhancing productivity and innovation.** By leveraging AI-driven solutions, businesses can streamline processes, automate routine tasks and unlock valuable insights, empowering people to focus on high-impact work and stay ahead in a rapidly changing digital landscape.

- **Welcome an inter-generational workforce.** Recognising the unique strengths and perspectives that people from different age groups bring to the table can open the door to business innovation.

#1. Create a culture of shoshin

As business leaders and owners, start with you. You need to lead the way. Do you approach each situation with a willingness to learn and an open mind, regardless of your experience or expertise? This mindset promotes innovation and helps people avoid complacency, so modelling the behaviour yourself may encourage others to follow suit.

If you already have a culture of shoshin in your business, that is great. If not, let the following suggestions help you reflect and take action towards developing a shoshin culture:

- Create an environment where people feel free to explore new possibilities and ask 'Why?' or 'What if?' questions.

- Be mindful and be more in the present moment, which allows for more shoshin thinking.

- Break down complex problems into manageable parts. This aligns with the Zen concept of simplicity and clarity.

- Be flexible and willing to adjust your thinking based on new information or changing circumstances that arise.

- Have more patience and try and understand that meaningful change and growth take time and effort and may not happen in the time frame you desire.

- Act with clear intent and purpose.

- Set a positive example for your business by consistently practising shoshin.

- Discuss reflection with your people. By creating an environment where people feel encouraged to examine their thoughts and actions, leaders can prompt their people to see if they are living the shoshin way. Have regular discussions or workshops focused on the concept of shoshin, where people are invited to share their reflections on how they approach tasks, challenges and learning opportunities.

- Practise humility by being open to new ideas. Look for that nugget of genius!

- Mix capabilities by getting a group of people with a variety of experience and watch innovative approaches unroll.

A great book on this topic is called *Zen Mind, Beginner's Mind* by Shunryu Suzuki. This book is rooted in Zen Buddhism and has implications for both business practices and the use of a shoshin mindset among people in business.

Instead of being stuck doing things the same way, the shoshin mindset enables people to stay open to new ideas, be more adaptable to change and be better able to respond to the ever-changing, dynamic business environment.

This mindset encourages continual learning and growth, which can lead to more creative solutions and a more vibrant, resilient business.

Be like Hiroshi. Let go of assumptions and be like an empty cup, ready to be filled with new insights and ideas.

#2. Embrace technology like artificial intelligence (AI)

The pace of AI development is staggering, with new breakthroughs and advancements emerging weekly. There are many small-to-medium businesses that are ignoring AI — but it is here to stay. However, AI can't develop a shoshin mentality.

Business leaders and owners that are embracing technology have a shoshin mindset. Early in 2018, Sundar Pichai, the CEO of Alphabet Inc. (Google's parent company), remarked that AI is one of the most important things humanity is working on and that it is more profound than electricity or fire. He discussed AI's potential to fundamentally change how we conduct work and how it can enhance our lives in various ways, from health to education to how we process information. Pichai's observations underscore the transformative impact AI is expected to have on society and the economy, akin to the revolution brought about by electricity in the past century.

Approaching AI with a beginner's mind allows people to stay agile and receptive to new ideas and technologies. This adaptability is essential for leveraging the full potential of AI.

People from various backgrounds, not just those with a traditional computer science background, can contribute meaningfully to AI applications. A beginner's mindset encourages people to explore and integrate knowledge from different domains.

As AI technologies become increasingly accessible, it is essential for people to have a basic understanding of its potential. A beginner's mindset promotes a willingness to learn and experiment, ensuring that people can harness the power of AI. This is particularly relevant as AI applications integrate into various aspects of daily life, from healthcare to finance, education and others.

At the same time, certain professions, like healthcare, counselling and education, require empathy and genuine human connection. AI can assist in some aspects but cannot replace the deep emotional understanding that humans can build with one another.

Empathy is not the only thing that limits AI. Here are some other parts of human cognition and creativity that AI cannot replicate:

- AI can assist in generating ideas based on patterns and data, but it lacks the ability to think creatively, challenge the status quo or come up with truly innovative solutions. People that are shoshin thinkers can approach problems from multiple angles and connect concepts.

- AI operates based on algorithms and data, but it lacks moral and ethical judgement. Shoshin thinkers can evaluate the potential consequences of AI decisions, considering both the short-term and long-term impacts on society, and make ethical choices.

- AI often struggles with understanding context and nuance. Shoshin thinkers can take into account the broader social, cultural and historical context when making decisions.

- While AI can learn from data and adapt to rules, it cannot demonstrate true curiosity or a shoshin mentality — being open to new experiences and learning from them.

When AI systems make mistakes or cause harm, accountability becomes a crucial issue. Critical thinkers can assess the causes of AI errors and determine the appropriate actions to address them.

#3. Be open to having an inter-generational workforce

In a time when a multigenerational workforce (up to five generations in the workforce for the first time in history) is becoming increasingly common, businesses find themselves at a historic juncture. For the first time in history, it is possible to have up to five different generations working side by side: Veterans, Baby Boomers, Generation X and Millennials, and now even Generation Z is making an entry into the workforce. Each generation brings a unique set of values, communication styles and work ethics, all shaped by the societal and technological landscapes that prevailed during their formative years.

For business leaders and owners, navigating these different generations with their own ideas, values and even preferred ways of communicating can be 'tricky', and the key part is knowing how to communicate and inspire each of the generations.

The five workplace generations can be broadly defined, though these definitions rely on a few generalisations and so they don't apply to individual circumstances:

- **Veterans (born up to 1945):** This generation typically had one job (a 'job for life') and their learning was through education and on-the-job training. While they may rarely feature in the workplace these days, Joe Biden is one example of an active Veteran in the workforce! Veterans add another layer of richness to the workplace tapestry with their discipline, leadership skills and unique perspectives.

- **Baby Boomers (born 1946–64):** This generation saw significant changes in society and were open to lifelong learning and adapting to new technologies. They typically have one to two jobs during the course of their career.

- **Generation X (born 1965–80):** This generation saw the technological advances of personal computing and the advent of the internet, and is the first generation to learn through self-help books. They often move between jobs and industries and understand the concept of continual learning.

- **Millennials (born 1981–96):** This generation grew up in the digital age and willingly adapt to technology. They value continuous learning and seek personal development opportunities. They are more likely to change jobs and industries multiple times in their careers.

- **Generation Z (born 1997–2012):** This generation prioritises digital learning platforms. They prefer online resources like videos, apps, interactive games and ebooks for acquiring new information or skills. They lean towards self-directed learning on platforms such as YouTube, Coursera and Khan Academy where knowledge is on-demand and self-paced.

My dad, a Baby Boomer, had one career. For me, as a member of Generation X, I have changed my career three times already, from engineer, to business leader, to business owner and founder.

Generation Z (the same generation as my kids) is likely to have a minimum of six careers in their life, according to most universities and generational studies.

To cultivate an effective inter-generational workplace culture, businesses must create an environment of mutual respect where different generations appreciate and leverage their distinct strengths.

Clear communication approaches, diverse team structures and tailored training programs are essential. Business leaders and owners must be inclusive and adept at bridging generational divides, promoting programs such as cross-generational mentoring to facilitate bidirectional learning.

Flexible work arrangements and personalised recognition can meet the diverse needs and motivational drivers of each age group. Above all, a culture that offers continual feedback and values each individual's contributions is crucial for fostering unity and ensuring all employees, regardless of age, feel valued and engaged in their work.

The key is that everyone in the workplace is willing to continue to learn and upgrade their learning, much as you would update your business's computer or phone hardware or software.

As Alvin Toffler, the renowned futurist, once said, 'The illiterate of the 21st century will not be those who cannot read and write, but those who cannot learn, unlearn and relearn.'

As business leaders and owners, we need to know how to 'tap into' the mindset of the different generations to keep each generation engaged and also to encourage each generation to have the shoshin mentality. As your business navigates change, your people in different generations can be agile to do the same.

Business leaders and owners can optimise their inter-generational workforce in three main ways:

- **Promote cross-generational learning.** Encourage people from different generations to share their knowledge and expertise. Create opportunities where younger generations can learn from the experience of older generations and vice versa. Foster an environment of mutual respect and a willingness to learn from one another.

- **Offer flexible training and development.** Offer a range of training and development programs that cater to different generations. This would include face-to-face training as well as online training.

- **Provide regular feedback.** Implement a feedback system that allows people to provide input on their learning and growth needs. This feedback can be used to change training and development initiatives to better serve people of all generations (Chapter 4 talks more about the importance of giving and receiving feedback).

Harnessing the collective potential of a multigenerational workforce is not only essential for diversity and inclusion but also for innovation, productivity and adaptability.

Each generation brings a set of unique skills, perspectives and experiences to the table.

Baby Boomers may offer decades of industry knowledge and stability, while Generation X is known for its adaptability and entrepreneurial spirit. Millennials and Generation Z can guide the workplace with technological savvy, fresh ideas and a focus on social responsibility.

To harness the power of this diversity, leaders must create an inclusive work culture that values the strengths of each generation.

Case study: Toyota

As a leading Japanese automotive manufacturer, Toyota, like other manufacturers, was always trying to find the competitive edge.

In my view, Toyota applied shoshin into lean manufacturing and its Toyota Production System (TPS), and worked on every element of eliminating waste. The business focused on empowering people to identify and address problems at their source, resulting in significant time and cost savings.

Toyota's dedication to a beginner's mindset led to high levels of quality. It encouraged people to detect and correct defects early in the production process, leading to lower defect rates and increased customer satisfaction.

Toyota's approach to continuous improvement promotes a culture of people involvement and engagement. People are encouraged to suggest improvements and take ownership of their work processes.

Toyota's beginner's mindset has resulted in a culture of cost control and waste reduction. This approach has contributed to the business's strong financial performance and consistent profitability.

Toyota also allowed the principle of shoshin into its TPS by making jidoka a part of the system. Jidoka is a principle that empowers people who work as operators to automatically stop production when a defect is detected for early problem identification and resolution, which enables each person to adopt a shoshin mentality as well.

Case study: Netflix

I believe that Netflix is a great example of a business that may be using shoshin and AI. To maintain its market leadership and maintain customer experience, Netflix uses AI algorithms to analyse user viewing habits, preferences and behaviours. The AI system continually adapts its recommendations, providing users with a personalised content selection. This approach has increased user engagement and retention.

Netflix maintains a culture of experimentation, encouraging its people to explore new technologies and strategies, even in areas where they might not be considered experts. The business continuously learns from user data, adapting its recommendations, features and content library to better serve its customers.

Case study: Amazon

Amazon is a great example of creating a culture of shoshin. Amazon has a set of 16 Leadership Principles that guide its culture. Principles like Customer Obsession, Invent and Simplify, and Learn and Be Curious reflect a commitment to shoshin.

Amazon hires for innovation, looking for qualities such as adaptability, customer thinking, and a willingness to learn and innovate.

Amazon actively encourages people to explore new ideas, even if they fail. And as a result, they have come up with initiatives like Amazon Web Services (AWS) and the Kindle e-reader.

Amazon also invests heavily in training its people, providing a wide range of programs for people to build upon their skills and keep learning.

Reflections

Before diving into the questions that follow, ensure you have a journal and a pen within reach to capture your thoughts. Refer to Chapter 1 if you need a reminder on how to create the ideal setting for these reflections about your business. Consider the questions and journal your answers. Remember, you may also like to ask the people in your business to reflect on the same questions.

The questions are broken down into several sections. Separating the questions into distinct areas allows for a more structured and focused approach to addressing each aspect of encouraging a shoshin mentality and lifelong learning. By breaking down the discussion into specific topics, we can go deeper into each area, explore relevant questions, and develop actionable insights and strategies. This approach facilitates a more detailed way of looking at important aspects. Additionally, the discussion into separate sections helps maintain clarity and coherence, making it easier for you to track progress and identify areas for further exploration or improvement.

Assessing for a shoshin mindset during hiring:

- How do you assess a person's openness to learning during the hiring process?

- What specific strategies do you use to identify people with a shoshin mindset?

Encouraging a shoshin mentality:

- How do you currently foster a shoshin mentality among key people?

- Can you think of specific examples of situations where encouraging a beginner's mindset led to positive outcomes?

Catering to different generations:

- What specific initiatives or training programs do you tailor to different generational preferences?

- How do you ensure that learning opportunities are inclusive and accessible to all age groups within the business?

Allowing mistakes as part of the business's culture:

- How are mistakes perceived and managed within the business?

- Can you think of examples where mistakes led to valuable insights or improvements?

Encouraging lifelong learning initiatives:

- What are the ongoing education initiatives currently in place?

- How do you communicate the value of continuous learning to people?

Creating feedback mechanisms for learning initiatives:

- How are lifelong learning initiatives measured and assessed?

- What mechanisms do you have in place for people to provide (and/or receive) feedback on learning initiatives?

Creating incentives for lifelong learning:

- What existing incentive programs do you have that motivate people to engage in ongoing education?

- What potential improvements or additional incentives could further encourage a culture of continuous improvement?

Communicating strategically:

- How do you communicate the importance of continuous learning to people?

- How do you as a business leader or owner set an example and reinforce the business's commitment to lifelong learning?

Summary

In conclusion, the three key actions outlined — fostering a culture of shoshin, embracing technology like artificial intelligence (AI), and understanding and catering to different generational learning styles — provide an approach for business leaders and owners to address shoshin in the current ever-changing environment we work in.

Fostering a culture of shoshin involves embracing a beginner's mindset, promoting innovation and fostering an environment of continuous learning. Business leaders and owners need to lead by example, encouraging flexibility, patience, and a focus on simplicity and clarity.

This mindset, exemplified by leaders like Toyota, Netflix and Amazon, has been shown to drive continuous improvement and adaptability.

The integration of technology, especially AI, is crucial for staying competitive. However, it's important to acknowledge that AI lacks the creative and ethical aspects of human thinking. Business leaders and owners need to approach AI with a shoshin mentality.

Lastly, recognising and catering to different generational learning styles is essential in today's multigenerational workforce. Leaders need to understand and promote inter-generational training. There are many things each generation can learn from the next.

Summary

CHAPTER 6
THE BEST OF BOTH WORLDS

Creating a culture of diversity and inclusion

Diversity refers to the presence of a variety of different characteristics, attributes, backgrounds and perspectives within a business or community. These differences can include race, ethnicity, gender, age, sexual orientation, religion, physical abilities, cultural backgrounds and education.

Diversity is more than just a buzzword. For me, diversity is about having people in your team that think differently.

Embracing diversity means recognising and valuing the uniqueness of each individual, being respectful and appreciating their differences. Diversity is not just a matter of representation but also an acknowledgment of the different viewpoints and experiences that people bring.

If you have experienced different cultures in your business, you may have witnessed the magic that occurs when people with diverse backgrounds work on certain initiatives and projects. It is essential for business leaders and owners to take action to incorporate diversity into their businesses if they want to fully appreciate and experience this magic.

Inclusivity is ensuring that all people, regardless of their backgrounds, characteristics, abilities or circumstances, are provided with equal opportunities, access and treatment. It is the principle where everyone feels welcome, respected and able to fully participate.

This chapter is about encouraging you to own everything about yourself — your past, present and future — and also honour the people in your business who have different backgrounds. You are celebrating both the personal and professional diversity that people bring into your business with them — the kind of diversity that has become part of their DNA.

As business leaders and owners, you want to incorporate the 'whole' of the person into your business. You want people to bring the best of the cultures that they've worked in — whether it's come from their families, whether it's come from the businesses that they've worked for, whether it's come from certain friends — and you want to bring that into the culture in your business and create a 'melting pot'.

Having diverse people working in your business brings many benefits (besides the fact that it is the right thing to do!):

- When diverse people work within your business, it allows you to see the bigger picture and address market trends before they emerge. This is like finding a bucket of gold!

- Diverse perspectives and backgrounds in the business can lead to more creativity and innovation. It enables your business to adapt to the global marketplace. By drawing from the richness of multiple cultures, your business can create an environment where people think outside the box. When people approach challenges from various angles, they are more likely to generate a variety of ideas and solutions. Innovation thrives in an environment of diverse thinking.

- Different cultures approach problem-solving in diverse ways. Based on this, you can encourage your people to collaborate and use their complementary skills to find better solutions and make better decisions. These diverse perspectives allow people to consider a broader range of potential solutions.

- Different thinking styles can reveal hidden opportunities and uncover blind spots.

- When people from diverse backgrounds contribute their insights, it reduces the risk of 'groupthink' (everyone forming one view) and ensures that decisions are based on the multitude of views from the diverse people in front of you, not just one or two of the loudest voices.

- People with diverse thinking can pivot more effectively when circumstances change. Their ability to draw on a wide range of perspectives allows them to respond to unexpected challenges and find new opportunities.

A business that values diversity in thinking is more likely to attract and retain top people. People feel valued when their unique perspectives are recognised and appreciated, leading to higher job satisfaction and engagement.

You might already be a business leader and owner who is aware of the importance of diverse backgrounds and what people bring with them, and who is driven by how to cultivate a positive and diverse culture that encourages people to bring all their past learnings into the present. But if this is an area that you have been hearing a lot about but are unsure on how to cultivate a diverse and inclusive culture, hopefully this chapter gives you one or two actions you can take.

Research that supports diversity and inclusion

According to the 2020 McKinsey & Company report 'Diversity Wins', businesses with diverse executive teams are more likely to outperform their peers on profitability. The report analysed data from over 1000 companies across 15 countries.

An article published in 2016 in the *Harvard Business Review* ('Why diverse teams are smarter' by David Rock and Heidi Grant) suggests that diverse teams are more innovative. A study conducted by the Boston Consulting Group and published in 2018 found that companies with diverse management teams reported higher levels of revenue from new products and services (their gauge of innovation).

A study by the Peterson Institute for International Economics found a positive correlation between the presence of women in leadership positions and firm performance. Companies with at least 30 per cent women in leadership positions had net profit margins that were 6 percentage points higher than companies with no women in leadership roles.

The 2018 *Deloitte Review* article 'The diversity and inclusion revolution' by Juliet Bourke and Bernadette Dillon shows that an inclusive culture contributes to higher levels of people engagement and productivity. Inclusive businesses are more likely to attract and retain top talent.

Businesses that create diversity in their thinking and leadership roles, are often viewed more favourably by the public and can build a better brand as a result. They are more favoured by potential partners and suppliers. This brand reputation can lead to increased opportunities for collaboration and growth.

A story from my own life

When I arrived in Australia from India at the age of 11, I didn't know whether I fit into the Indian culture or Australian culture. I spoke very good English, but I had a very heavy Indian accent.

As a result of that, a couple of the kids at school made fun of me and called me all sorts of horrible names. It was the first time in my life I realised that I was different. At the tender age of 11, all I wanted to do was to be able to leave my skin colour and my culture behind so that I could fit into my new country and culture.

One of the things I did was try to mask my Indian accent and put on an Australian accent. I tried not to speak Hindi with my family at home. In fact, I asked my family, much to their disappointment, not to speak to me in Hindi because I needed to improve my Australian accent. Nor were there many Indian families in our Australian country town. For a while, it became very important to me that I had more Australian (or Aussie, as we call it!) friends or spent time with people that had Australian accents. This was just one of the things that I did to try and fit in.

During this period, I was still living what felt like a 'double' life. I was practising Indian cultural rituals while at the same time wanting to be an Aussie!

Every day, we would hold a prayer (or puja) in our house. When I had exams, my mum and dad would put a little black mark on me to prevent any evil thoughts or evil spirits coming towards me. I would try and hide it on my hair rather than my skin for the fear of not wanting to look like a weirdo.

Every year we would celebrate 'Rakhi' (which is an Indian festival between a brother and a sister), 'Diwali' (which is the equivalent of the Indian Christmas also called the Festival of Lights) and 'Holi' (the festival of colour). We would celebrate so many other festivals too, like not eating eggs for nine days in the Navaratri.

Because I just wanted to be able to fit in and I didn't want any Indian food cooked when my friends came around for a playdate or a birthday party, I used to try and hide that part of myself from others and, to be honest, from myself.

As I grew up past my teens and into my twenties, I realised that there are some parts of the Australian culture which I found very challenging and felt they were not aligned to my values. A lot of the kids I knew when I went to their house for a playdate yelled at their parents. Some even swore at their parents. And I thought that this was really disrespectful. Families seemed to be a lot more fragmented. And even though I sometimes longed for Aussie parents who would not control me, I realised there were some benefits to being taken care of by my family in their way.

I was also clear that I wanted to marry an Aussie. Someone not only who I loved but who would give me the freedom to be myself in my future.

The standing joke in our family is that after many robust conversations with my mum, I ended up falling in love with and marrying an Australian. Over time, I have discovered that he loves everything Indian — in many ways, he is more Indian than me. He loves Indian culture. He is currently reading the *Bhagavad Gita*, which is the Indian holy book. My parents love him and treat him like their son. He jokes with me that whatever you resist, persists!

When I was pregnant with our daughter, my husband wanted to name her Shanti. And I remember saying to him that Shanti's spelling and pronunciation is very close to my name, Shivani. I didn't think that it was a great idea. Anyway, he's a meditator and a yogi, as well as a HR director. And he really wanted to name her Shanti.

So, our daughter is called Shanti, which means peace and is a 5000-year name. And when I was pregnant with our son, he said to me, 'Wouldn't it be beautiful to be able to call him Om?' I thought to myself, 'Who is this guy?'

Om Shanti is a very old chant that is recited today by hundreds of millions of people each day at the start or at the end of their yoga or meditation practice at the start of their day. I know this as I grew up doing it most days!

And so came the names of our children — Om and Shanti. I have been asked many times if I am religious because people assume I named the kids. The kids joke that they've got an Indian dad and an Aussie mum, even though it is the other way around.

We celebrate a number of festivals that are important to us. And now that we've been together for almost 20 years, we celebrate Rakhi and Diwali as well as the Australian festivals. There are parts of Australian culture we both love. We love celebrating our Christmas. We love celebrating the AFL Grand Final day with veggie sausage rolls (we are all vegetarian now!). What we have tried to do is take both our cultures and all the things we love about these cultures and blend them into one.

It took me to a long time to honour my culture and my past. When I did, I became a more balanced person, a better partner and mum, and also a better business leader and owner.

My culture and my past are now represented in all of my businesses. Part of their profits go towards educating girls in India and other developing countries. A picture of an Indian girl has been on my vision board for over a decade, and I share that with my management and leadership team.

As a business leader and owner, you have that opportunity to honour the past, present and future of your people.

Indra Nooyi

Indra Nooyi, the former CEO of PepsiCo, is known for her strong commitment to diversity and inclusion within the business. During her tenure as CEO from 2006 to 2018, she implemented several initiatives and strategies to promote diversity and inclusion at all levels of the business.

Nooyi actively promoted diversity in the leadership team by appointing people from various backgrounds and underrepresented groups to key executive positions. Under her leadership, PepsiCo's executive team became more diverse in terms of gender, race and ethnicity.

Nooyi introduced performance metrics that tied executive compensation to diversity and inclusion goals. This incentivised leaders to take concrete actions to increase diversity within the business.

She established a global diversity and inclusion council to oversee the business's diversity and inclusion initiatives. The council was responsible for setting priorities and driving change in this area.

Nooyi also sought out diverse suppliers, including women-owned, minority-owned and veteran-owned businesses. This helped support and promote diversity throughout PepsiCo's supply chain.

Nooyi encouraged a culture of inclusivity by promoting understanding and acceptance of different cultures and backgrounds. She believed that a more inclusive culture would lead to more innovation and a better understanding of diverse consumer markets.

She established mentorship and development programs to help underrepresented people advance in their careers. These programs aimed to provide guidance and support for people to reach their full potential.

Nooyi supported and encouraged the growth of People Resource Groups at PepsiCo. These groups allowed people to come together based on shared backgrounds or interests, fostering a sense of belonging and support within the business.

Under her leadership, PepsiCo's marketing campaigns often celebrated diversity and inclusivity. This was reflected in advertising that embraced different cultures, backgrounds and communities.

I had the privilege of interviewing Indra for the Entrepreneurs' Organization (EO) as part of the Powerhouse series. She was incredible for the hour I interviewed her and her stories and focus on diversity and inclusion were inspiring. You can find this interview on the EO website (please note that you have to be an EO member to access the interview).

Examples of businesses addressing diversity

Many modern businesses recognise the importance of factoring diversity into the way they work. Here are just two examples:

- **Google** has created a culture of innovation and collaboration by actively seeking diverse perspectives and celebrating individuality. Google's annual 'Googlegeist' survey demonstrates its commitment to its people and a blended, inclusive culture. Inclusive environments empower people to contribute their insights; effective collaboration thrives on open communication channels; and diversity ensures a range of perspectives and approaches within teams.

- **Salesforce**'s commitment to social responsibility and philanthropy has contributed to a blended culture that values community engagement. Salesforce's '1-1-1' model, donating 1 per cent of equity, 1 per cent of product and 1 per cent of people's time to charitable causes, reflects its dedication to blending values with action.

Actions

To create a culture of diversity within your business, I recommend these three key actions:

- **Provide diversity training to all people in the business.** This training should focus on building awareness, understanding and empathy towards different backgrounds, experiences and perspectives. This way, you create a more inclusive and welcoming environment for everyone.

- **Embrace cultural celebrations and practices as part of your business culture.** Encourage people to share their traditions, customs and holidays, and provide opportunities for cross-cultural learning and appreciation. By celebrating diversity in this way, you demonstrate respect for all cultures and create a sense of belonging among your team members.

- **Promote diversity in leadership positions by actively seeking out and supporting candidates from underrepresented groups.** Create opportunities for diverse voices to be heard and represented at all levels of the business, including in decision-making roles.

#1. Provide appropriate diversity training

Diversity training for people typically covers a wide range of topics and aims to promote understanding, inclusivity and awareness of diversity-related issues. This training may involve some of the following topics for your business, depending on where on the diversity scale you are. Here are some ideas to implement this action:

- Defining diversity and explaining that it encompasses a broad spectrum of characteristics, including race, ethnicity, gender, age, sexual orientation, disability, religion and more.

- Addressing unconscious biases, which are automatic, unintentional and often based on stereotypes that can impact decision-making and behaviour.

- Discussing the concepts of inclusion and equity and how they relate to creating a fair and welcoming workplace for all people.

- Ensuring your managers and all your people are aware of anti-discrimination laws and regulations to ensure compliance.

- Recognising and respecting different gender identities and expressions and understanding the challenges faced by transgender and non-binary people.

- Promoting inclusivity for people of all sexual orientations and addressing stereotypes or biases related to LGBTQ+ people.

- Understanding the experiences and needs of people with disabilities, including accessibility and accommodations your business can make.

- Emphasising respect for diverse religious beliefs and practices in the workplace.

- Recognising the unique perspectives and characteristics of different generations (in other words, people who are Baby Boomers, Generation X, Millennials and Generation Z, as discussed in Chapter 5) and promoting inter-generational cooperation.

- Teaching people how to respond when they witness discrimination or harassment, which helps to promote a supportive work environment.

In my view, an example of a business leader and a business that has implemented diversity training well is Sundar Pichai from Google (Alphabet Inc.):

- Google offers mandatory unconscious bias training for all its people. This training aims to make people aware of the unconscious biases that can influence decision-making, hiring and interactions in the workplace.

- Google conducts inclusive leadership workshops for managers and leaders. These workshops focus on helping leaders champion diversity, promote inclusion and create equitable teams. Leaders are encouraged to lead by example and foster an inclusive culture within their teams.

- Google provides core diversity training to people. This training covers various aspects of diversity, including race, ethnicity, gender, sexual orientation and disability. It aims to create a more informed and empathetic workforce by addressing the experiences and challenges faced by underrepresented groups.

- Google has incorporated diversity training into its hiring processes. This includes training for recruiters and interviewers. The business actively seeks to increase the representation of underrepresented groups in its workforce.

#2. Embrace cultural celebrations and practices

As a business leader and owner, embracing cultural celebrations and practices is a meaningful way to promote diversity, inclusivity and cultural awareness within your business. Here are some ideas on how to implement this:

- Educate people about the significance of various cultural celebrations and practices. Provide information about the history, traditions and customs associated with these events.

- Acknowledge the cultural diversity within your business and express respect for different backgrounds. Encourage people to share their cultural traditions and practices and their stories about these.

- Develop and implement inclusive policies that support cultural diversity. This may include flexible scheduling to accommodate cultural holidays or dress code policies that respect cultural needs.

- Reflect cultural diversity in your marketing materials and product offerings. This may include creating products related to cultural celebrations, promoting cultural influencers and using diverse models in advertising.

- Recognise and celebrate cultural holidays and observances within the business. This can include decorations, special events, and sharing cultural foods and traditions.

- Ask for feedback from people to assess if the cultural celebrations and practices are effective, and use this feedback to improve.

- Set measurable diversity and inclusion goals related to cultural diversity, and celebrate achievements in meeting these goals.

- Foster effective communication in a diverse workplace by implementing training programs focused on language sensitivity, active listening techniques and clear, respectful dialogue, while also encouraging an inclusive culture where diverse perspectives are valued and respected. Additionally, creating opportunities for open discussions, providing feedback mechanisms and leading by example through your own communication practices can improve the effectiveness of communication in your business.

H&M, the global fashion retailer, has had great results from celebrating cultural events and traditions through its clothing collections and marketing campaigns. In some locations, H&M stores have been decorated to coincide with cultural celebrations. This might include special window displays, decorations and signage that align with the theme of the event. During Halloween season, retailers capitalise on the holiday's popularity by introducing themed products and decorations to attract people looking to celebrate. For example, major retailers like Walmart, Target and Party City offer costumes, decorations and party supplies.

#3. Promote diversity in leadership positions

I once worked with a leader of a business who spoke all the right words on diversity but deep down did not believe in it. As a result of his behaviours and actions, people felt excluded.

Not only did that business miss out on great people who could have stepped into a variety of leadership roles, but the business also caused its people to feel disengaged because they weren't working in a diverse culture.

Here are some steps that you as a business leader or owner can take to promote diversity and inclusion at the leadership level within your business:

- Define specific, measurable and time-bound diversity goals for leadership positions. Make these goals a part of your business's strategic plan.

- Involve diverse hiring panels in leadership selection processes. Multiple perspectives can help reduce bias and promote diversity.

- Establish mentorship and sponsorship programs that connect high-potential diverse people with senior leaders who can guide their career growth.

- Celebrate the achievements and contributions of diverse leaders within the business, setting them as role models.

In one of my businesses where I had a diverse group of people, some had grown up in cultures where it was not seen as appropriate to question authority so when I asked for feedback, I didn't receive any from these people. It took time for me to build trust with them and for them to know that when they did give feedback, there were not going to be any repercussions.

When these people started to share feedback, the insights really helped shape a better culture of the business, which I am so grateful for.

One of the insights we received came from a person in our team from an Iranian background. She shared that as someone newer to the country, she did not understand some of the abbreviations and slang Australian we used and she felt a bit silly asking what it meant. As a result, she felt excluded. When we discussed this with the managers, we ensured we used simple language so that she would feel included.

Case study: Salesforce

Salesforce, under the leadership of CEO Marc Benioff, has been promoting diversity in leadership positions. Salesforce is a global cloud computing business that has made diversity and inclusion core components of its corporate culture and business strategy.

Salesforce's executive team is diverse, with a strong representation of women and people from various backgrounds. Leaders like Tony Prophet, previously Chief Equality Officer, and Ebony Beckwith, Chief Business Officer and CEO of the Salesforce Foundation, have played key roles in shaping the business's diversity and inclusion initiatives.

Salesforce conducted a pay equity assessment and pledged to address any unexplained pay differences. The business has consistently maintained its commitment to equal pay for equal work, ensuring fairness and equity for all people.

Salesforce has diversity in its board of directors, with members representing a variety of backgrounds and experiences.

Salesforce supports Ohana Groups, which are its Employee Resource Groups (ERGs, or what I might call 'People Resource Groups'). These groups represent various dimensions of diversity, including those focused on Black, Latinx, LGBTQ+, women and more. Salesforce has adopted inclusive hiring practices, such as using tools and technologies to eliminate gender-biased language from job descriptions.

Salesforce leverages its philanthropic efforts and social impact programs to support diverse communities, with initiatives like the Salesforce 1-1-1 model, which is committed to donating products, resources and people time to support underprivileged communities.

CEO Marc Benioff is also known for being a voice for diversity and equal pay.

Reflections

Before diving into the questions that follow, ensure you have a journal and a pen within reach to capture your thoughts. Refer to Chapter 1 if you need a reminder on how to create the ideal setting for these reflections about your business. Consider the questions and journal your answers. Remember, you may also like to ask the people in your business to reflect on the same questions.

The questions are broken down into several sections. Separating the questions into distinct areas allows for a more structured and focused approach to addressing each aspect of creating a culture of diversity and inclusion. By breaking down the discussion into specific topics, we can go deeper into each area, explore relevant questions, and develop actionable insights and strategies. This approach facilitates a more detailed way of looking at important aspects. Additionally, the discussion into separate sections helps maintain clarity and coherence, making it easier for you to track progress and identify areas for further exploration or improvement.

Evaluating your vision and commitment:

- How would you describe your vision for diversity and inclusion within your business?

- Can you see the strategic importance of diversity and inclusion in achieving your business goals?

Committing to diversity through leadership:

- As a business leader and owner, how do you personally demonstrate a commitment to diversity and inclusion?

- What steps have you taken to create an inclusive leadership style that values diverse perspectives?

Engaging people:

- How do you gauge the level of people engagement in diversity and inclusion initiatives?

- Can you share examples of successful initiatives that have positively impacted people engagement?

Measuring progress:

- What metrics or key performance indicators do you use to measure the success of diversity and inclusion efforts?

- How do you track progress over time and make adjustments based on the data?

Addressing unconscious bias:

- How do you address unconscious bias within your business, especially in decision-making processes?

- Have you implemented any training or awareness programs to change biases among people?

Developing inclusive leadership:

- How are you developing and promoting inclusive leadership skills within the leadership team?

- What resources or programs are in place to ensure leaders at all levels embrace diversity in their decision-making?

Establishing People Resource Groups:

- Do you encourage and support the establishment of People Resource Groups?

- How do these groups contribute to a more inclusive workplace culture?

Recruiting and retaining people:

- How has the business evolved its recruitment strategies to attract a diverse talent pool?

- What retention strategies are in place to ensure a diverse workforce is engaged?

Championing diversity in supply chains:

- How do you prioritise diversity and inclusion in the selection of suppliers and partners?

- How can the business leverage its influence to encourage diversity throughout the supply chain?

Gathering feedback:

- How do you collect feedback from people regarding the effectiveness of diversity and inclusion initiatives?

- In what ways are people encouraged to provide input on shaping the business's approach to diversity and inclusion?

Handling challenges:

- Can you think of an example of a challenge or resistance faced in promoting diversity and inclusion, and how was it addressed?

- What strategies do you employ to navigate potential obstacles in advancing diversity and inclusion?

Summary

The leadership of Indra Nooyi at PepsiCo stands as a testament to the power of commitment to diversity and inclusion. Throughout her 12-year tenure as CEO, Nooyi implemented a comprehensive set of initiatives to promote diversity at every level of the business. From diversifying the executive team to tying compensation to diversity goals and establishing a global diversity and inclusion council, her strategic approach has become a model for fostering a culture of inclusivity.

The recommended actions show the importance of continuous efforts to promote diversity and inclusion within businesses. By providing appropriate diversity training, embracing cultural celebrations and actively promoting diversity in leadership positions, businesses can cultivate environments that value individual differences and contribute to overall success.

The examples of successful implementation by companies like Google, H&M and Salesforce demonstrate the positive impact these actions can have on business culture and performance.

As businesses increasingly recognise the importance of blending values with action, the integration of diversity and inclusion initiatives becomes not only a reflection of ethical principles but a key driver of sustained success to attract and retain the right people in your business.

CHAPTER 7
MANAGERS AS COACHES

Empowering your managers to coach your people

If your managers are able to coach their people rather than always be in the directive role, it creates more engagement and empowerment of your people. People are more likely to stay with a business where a manager is investing in their development. Coaching can contribute to higher retention of people.

Coaching enables managers to help their people identify strengths and weaknesses and work on improving their skills and performance. Through regular feedback and guidance, people can make progress and meet their goals. When managers provide people with opportunities for learning and growth, it helps them acquire new skills and knowledge.

Coaching involves regular, constructive feedback. Effective communication between managers and their people is essential for understanding expectations of the work that is required and making adjustments.

Managers can use coaching to help people achieve their goals. Coaching can enhance and develop a range of skills in managers and their people, such as:

- **Motivation and focus.** Effective coaching by managers can boost people's motivation and focus, and when people understand how their work contributes to the business's wider goals (so they have a shared vision), this can also enhance motivation and focus (Chapter 1 explores the importance of a shared vision further). When people receive guidance and support from their managers, they are more likely to feel engaged and committed to their work.

- **Conflict resolution.** Managers rely on their coaching skills when resolving conflicts and improving relationships within the team. Managers who can mediate and facilitate communication can prevent conflict and address issues effectively.

- **Leadership development.** Coaching skills allows managers to identify people with high potential and prepare them for leadership roles. In this chapter, I also want to explore the various types of coaching conversations and coaching techniques, and their impact on the development of your people.

Amelia the coach

To illustrate the importance of the 'manager as coach' and 'employee' relationship, consider the example of Amelia and Alex.

Amelia was known throughout the business for her coaching abilities. Amelia understood the power of coaching and its transformative effect on her team members.

Amelia received a new team member, Alex, who was skilled but was reserved and unsure how to communicate or develop his own potential.

She saw the potential in Alex and knew that investing time and effort into helping him build his confidence would really pay off down the road. First off, it would make him feel good about himself and what he's doing. As he gets better, he'll have more chances at getting good jobs or starting his own thing. Plus, he'll be able to work more effectively and efficiently. And when he feels confident, he might come up with cool new ideas or ways to do things. As he faces challenges and learns from them, he'll get stronger and be able to handle tough times better. And as he becomes more sure of himself, he might end up leading others or working with them in cool new ways. Plus, feeling good about himself will make him better at connecting with people and working together. So, it's not just about him—it's about making everything better for him and everyone around him too.

Amelia began with active listening, asking open-ended questions to understand Alex's aspirations and goals. She wanted to know what motivated him and what he hoped to achieve. Alex, initially reserved, gradually opened up and shared his ambitions to excel in project management and leadership.

Amelia tailored her coaching approach to support Alex's development. She provided regular feedback, highlighting his strengths and offering constructive guidance on areas that needed improvement. Amelia encouraged him to take ownership of his projects, allowing him to apply his skills and learn from his experiences.

(continued)

Amelia also provided Alex with opportunities to learn and grow. She encouraged him to attend relevant workshops, training sessions and conferences. She even connected him with a mentor who had a successful track record in project management.

Amelia's coaching went beyond professional development. She recognised the importance of work-life balance and wellbeing. She supported Alex in setting achievable goals and maintaining a healthy balance between his personal life and work.

Over time, Alex's confidence grew and his performance accelerated. He not only excelled in project management but also began mentoring other team members.

Alex was offered a promotion, which he gladly accepted. He was grateful for the coaching and support he had received from Amelia.

Bill Campbell the trillion dollar coach

Bill Campbell's work made a big mark on me when I read the 2019 book *Trillion Dollar Coach: The Leadership Playbook of Silicon Valley's Bill Campbell* by Eric Schmidt, Jonathan Rosenberg and Alan Eagle. His legacy is a big story with a few main parts. First, there are his leadership ideas. He believed in things like trust, building good relationships and caring about people more than money. These ideas are still important for leaders today.

Then, there's his coaching style. His coaching methods are shared in the book, so anyone can learn from them. He showed that good coaching can make a huge difference.

Campbell also shaped the culture of businesses like Google and Apple. He focused on teamwork and making sure every person felt valued.

This helped these businesses become great places to work and led to lots of innovation.

Trillion Dollar Coach is all about his life and how he influenced others. It inspired me at a deep level. And his legacy lives on through the people he coached and the ideas he shared. They keep using his methods and spreading his wisdom, making sure his impact lasts a long time. This made me want to do more speaking, coaching and authoring.

Bill Campbell's unique coaching style extended to a wide range of influential tech leaders and executives, including Steve Jobs (Apple), Eric Schmidt (Google) and Jeff Bezos (Amazon):

- He provided coaching to Steve Jobs during Apple's various stages, helping to improve the business's operations and teamwork.

- He coached Eric Schmidt at Google and was the chairman of Google's board of directors. He worked with Eric to provide valuable counsel during Google's rapid growth phase.

- Bill Campbell was a personal mentor to Jeff Bezos at Amazon. His coaching played a role in shaping Amazon's corporate culture and leadership principles.

- Campbell coached Sheryl Sandberg during her time at Google and later at Facebook, contributing to her success and leadership.

He genuinely cared about the wellbeing and success of the leaders he coached. This personal touch was a hallmark of his coaching style.

He focused on *trust* as a pillar of his coaching. Campbell created a safe and confidential space where the people he coached could share their challenges and concerns. He was empathetic, non-judgemental and made leaders feel comfortable seeking guidance.

He was *results-oriented*. He helped the people he coached to set ambitious goals and provided the guidance and support they needed to achieve those goals.

He was known for his *direct communication*. He was not afraid to provide constructive feedback or challenge his coachees when necessary.

He helped leaders *define their leadership styles* and ensure that they were in alignment with their personal values and the values of their businesses.

He had great skills to *mediate and resolve conflicts*. His guidance helped improve communication and understanding among executives in the tech world.

His approach to coaching focused on fostering a *culture of collaboration* within a business.

His work with so many of the tech giants in Silicon Valley is why he is called the trillion dollar coach.

Examples of businesses embracing the manager as coach concept

Increasing numbers of businesses are investing in coaching training for their managers, with a focus on everything from general wellbeing to leadership diversity coaching. Here are two companies that value the manager as coach concept:

- **Google** believes in managers acting more like coaches. The company encourages managers to talk to their team members, ask questions and really listen to what they have to say. When a Google manager acts like a coach, they help their team members learn and grow. They don't just boss them around. Instead, they give them support and guidance to help them do better at their jobs and reach their goals. By having managers who are also coaches, Google makes sure that everyone in the team has a chance to learn and get better. This creates a friendly and helpful work environment where everyone can do their best work and feel supported along the way.

- **Verizon**, listed at No. 18 on LinkedIn's Top Companies list in 2022, has invested heavily in coaching, offering such services to its leaders to support career transitions, succession and specific performance goals.

Small to medium-sized businesses and coaching

The following real-life and lived-in examples come from some of the people I've had the privilege to work with and who have been willing to share their experiences of coaching in the workplace. I asked the question: 'What do you do to encourage your managers to take on coaching roles and actively support the development of their people members?' Here are their answers.

- **Jane Save, The Save Group:** 'We train them on how to conduct productive and motivating performance reviews and to provide daily feedback.'

- **Wes Blundy, Curvy:** 'We do this in quarterly conversations but have room for improvement here.'

- **Scott Orpin, MEGT:** 'I coach them — asking open questions which gets them to think about options and solutions.'

- **Kate Winter, Champion Web:** 'Communicate what is working and what is not working with the management process/system and showing that work can be done to a higher level when they take on more of a coaching role.'

- **Ali Koschel, Hunter New England and Central Coast Primary Health Network (HNECC PHN):** 'Work with them to identify strengths in themselves and in their people as a first point and encourage them to use good coaching methods to get the best out of their people.'

- **Nancy Youssef, Classic Mentoring:** 'Spent a lot of time helping with getting my second in charge to develop as a coach. Invested in her completing the Cert IV in TAA to become a certified trainer/facilitator.'

- **Sam Mathers, Fitter Futures**: 'I mentor and coach my leadership team about managing other team members and helping them to develop and improve. We have a "no blame" culture.'

- **Nicole Bryant, The Macro Group:** 'All managers have a weekly check in with each people member.'

- **Kate Save, Be Fit Food:** 'We hire people who are self-motivated who are always looking to stretch themselves as coaches.'

Actions

To implement the manager as coach approach, it may help to try these four actions:

- **Provide coaching training for managers.** This ensures they have the necessary skills and tools to support their teams effectively.

- **Recognise that managers have multiple roles but coaching is central to their responsibilities.** Putting coaching into context gives managers the confidence they need to deliver great results.

- **Develop a consistent coaching model that is used across the entire business.** This ensures alignment between departments and promotes a culture of coaching at all levels.

- **Prioritise coaching for coachable people.** To get the best results, focus on your most engaged people!

#1. Provide coaching training for managers

My first action is to implement coaching training programs designed to teach your managers coaching skills and techniques. These programs may include workshops, courses, or online resources. Ensure the training is interactive and includes role playing (as much as people hate it) and practise sessions.

Managers need to be aware of the different types of coaching conversations they need to have with their people, which require different intentions or focus for the person they are coaching:

- **Performance feedback coaching** engages the manager in performance feedback conversations with their people. The manager provides specific, actionable feedback on a person's performance, highlighting strengths and areas for improvement.

- **Goal-setting coaching** aligns people's objectives with the business's goals. Managers work with people to set SMART (Specific, Measurable, Achievable, Relevant, Time-bound) goals that challenge and motivate them.

- **Career development coaching** focuses on people's long-term career aspirations and how the business can support them.

Managers help people identify their career paths within the business and create development plans to reach their goals.

- **Leadership coaching** focuses on developing leadership skills, including communication, decision-making and people management, for people who have the potential to be future leaders.

- **Mental health coaching** supports your people's mental health and work-life balance. This coaching is becoming more important and helps people manage stress and maintain a healthy work-life equilibrium. It may also encourage people to access a business's employee assistance program (EAP), which is managed by an external provider and offers employees short-term counselling services, referral services, work-life balance resources and customised tools to help them overcome challenges.

To be an effective coach, there are some principles of coaching that managers need to learn as well. These principles may not align with their natural style and so manager training should also involve practising these skills:

- Managers **practise active listening** during coaching sessions. They pay close attention to what people are saying, ask clarifying questions and provide empathetic responses. This creates trust and open communication.

- Managers and people **collaborate** to set specific goals and create action plans to achieve them. These plans include milestones and deadlines to track progress.

- Managers need to **provide feedback** not only on past performance but also on future improvements. Managers encourage people to think about how they can apply feedback to future tasks and projects. (Chapter 4 talks more about providing feedback.)

- Managers **lead by example**, demonstrating the behaviours and skills they expect from their people. This sets a positive tone for coaching relationships.

#2. Recognise that managers wear different 'hats' (but they always come back to coaching)

Managers need to work out how to get your business from A to B and the speed at which you will get there. As the business leader and owner, you decide to go from A to B in the first place and set the direction. (Chapter 1 talks more about setting this vision for the business.) For a manger to make all the decisions in their haste to get from A to B, they need to consider many factors.

A manager has many different hats to wear. They need to be able to adapt, depending on the situation and the needs of their people.

In the 'Scrum' approach, managers are expected to take on four primary roles to support their people:

- **Coaching** involves guiding people in their professional growth and development, helping them improve their skills and overcome challenges.

- **Mentoring** goes beyond coaching to provide more individual guidance and support, drawing from the manager's own experiences and expertise to help people navigate their careers.

- **Training** involves equipping people with the knowledge and skills they need to succeed in their roles, whether through formal training sessions or informal learning opportunities.

- **Facilitating** involves creating an environment that enables effective collaboration and decision-making within the team, removing obstacles and ensuring that processes run smoothly.

The manager, after doing one of these other roles, returns to coaching (Scrum, 2023).

Take an impartial stance	Provide expertise and advice
Facilitating	Training
Coaching	Mentoring

The Scrum Coaching Model

Managers need to return to coaching because it is the best way to empower your people. Coaching creates an environment where people feel valued and motivated to take ownership of their professional growth. Through coaching, managers guide people in identifying their strengths and areas for improvement.

I believe coaching is like 'teaching people to fish rather than giving them fish'. This powerful concept shows the importance of empowering people to become self-sufficient. Instead of providing temporary solutions or handouts, the manager uses coaching to give people the knowledge and skills they need to sustain themselves and not be dependent on them. This not only benefits the person in their personal and professional growth but also contributes to the overall success of the business.

Coaching is essential for managers because it offers personalised development tailored to each person's needs and strengths. Unlike training, which follows a standardised approach, coaching adapts to unique circumstances. It encourages people to take ownership of their growth journey, allowing accountability and initiative.

Coaching promotes autonomy and independence by guiding people to solve problems themselves. It creates a continuous learning culture where people seek feedback and opportunities for improvement.

Coaching also builds resilience and adaptability. Through open communication and empathy, managers strengthen relationships with their people, creating trust and collaboration. Coaching also drives performance improvement by providing targeted feedback and support.

While these four roles — coaching, mentoring, training and facilitating — each serve a different purpose, effective managers often find themselves switching between them as needed and always returning to coaching.

Coaching, however, remains a linchpin in the manager's toolkit. It's the key that unlocks people's potential by empowering them to learn, grow and adapt independently. Effective coaching involves active listening, asking probing questions and providing constructive feedback. It builds trust and rapport between the manager and people, creating a supportive and motivating atmosphere.

A manager's success is based on their ability to navigate between coaching, mentoring, training and facilitating roles. While each role has its distinct focus, coaching plays a central role in empowering people to take charge of their own development. Managers who master these roles create not only individual people success but also the success of the business as a whole.

#3. Develop a model that is used consistently in the business by everyone

Each coach brings their unique perspective, strengths and preferences to their coaching approach. People coach differently due to various factors such as their personality, communication style, beliefs, experiences and the context in which they operate. Also, the needs and preferences of the coachee also influence how the coaching process unfolds.

As each manager will coach differently, it is important to use one coaching model that everyone in the business can use. This has many benefits.

A single coaching model ensures that coaching practices are consistent throughout the business. It also creates a unified approach to coaching, which can be helpful for your managers and your people.

Managers and their people know what to expect from the coaching process when a single model is used. This clarity helps set clear expectations and gives transparency in the coaching relationship.

Managers and people become familiar with the chosen coaching model, which makes the coaching process more efficient and can lead to more productive coaching sessions.

Using one coaching model enables businesses to monitor and control the quality of coaching interactions.

New managers can be trained as coaches more effectively when there is a single coaching model in place. They can follow a structured approach and learn the necessary skills.

The use of a single coaching model allows for the measurement of coaching outcomes more accurately. It simplifies the process of assessing the impact of coaching on people development and performance.

People who receive coaching from different managers within the business will benefit from a consistent experience. They don't need to adapt to different coaching styles, making the process less confusing.

There are several coaching models besides the GROW Model (which I will discuss in the rest of this action) that are effective in facilitating the coaching process. Some of these include:

- **OSKAR:** This model focuses on solution-focused coaching. OSKAR stands for Outcome, Scaling, Know-how and Resources, Affirm and Action, and Review. It identifies solutions using strengths and resources to take action towards desired outcomes.

- **TGROW:** Similar to GROW, the TGROW Model adds a 'T' for Topic at the beginning. This modification helps to clarify the specific topic or issue that the coachee wants to address, providing a clear focus for the coaching session.

- **CLEAR:** CLEAR stands for Contracting, Listening, Exploring, Action, and Review. This model establishes a clear coaching contract, using active listening, exploring various perspectives and options, taking action and reviewing progress.

- **Co-Active Coaching:** Co-Active Coaching focuses on the coachee's agenda and the partnership between the coach and coachee. It involves deepening awareness, taking action and addressing core principles such as curiosity, empathy and empowerment.

- **Outcome-Based Coaching:** This model focuses on clarifying desired outcomes and aligning actions with those outcomes.

It involves exploring current reality, identifying barriers, setting specific and measurable goals, and creating action plans to achieve those goals.

While there are different coaching models available, I love the GROW (Goals, Reality, Options, Will) as it provides a clear structure. Coaches may adapt and personalise these models based on their own style and the specific needs of the coachee.

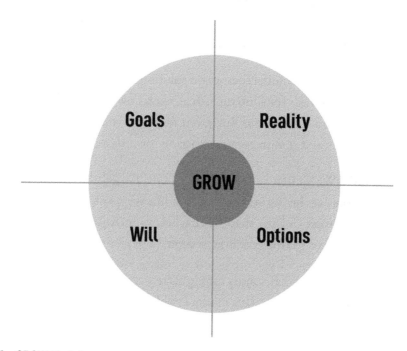

The GROW Model

The GROW Model includes four elements: Goals, Reality, Options and Will. It offers a clear approach to coaching conversations, enabling managers to help people clarify their goals, assess their current reality, explore options and commitment to taking action. People using the GROW Model gain a better understanding of their objectives and how to achieve them.

The GROW Model is a coaching tool created in the 1980s. It's a simple and effective way to help people reach their goals through coaching conversations. Max Landsberg, in his 1996 book *The Tao of Coaching*, gives some extra helpful ideas about why this model works well.

The GROW Model is about setting clear goals, understanding the current situation, exploring different options and making a plan to take action. It's like having a roadmap for your coaching journey.

Landsberg says that setting goals is crucial. These goals need to be specific, achievable and have a deadline. This gives you a clear target to aim for.

Understanding the current situation means looking at where you are right now. This includes figuring out what's working well and what challenges you're facing.

Exploring options is about brainstorming different ways to reach your goals. This is where creativity comes in, as you consider different paths to success.

Making a plan and committing to it is essential. This step ensures that the coaching conversation leads to action and progress toward your goals.

I like to use the GROW Model for the following reasons:

- **It is simple:** The GROW Model is easy to understand, making it accessible for both coaches and coachees.

- **It is versatile:** It can be applied to various coaching contexts, from personal development to professional goal-setting, making it adaptable to different situations.

- **It focuses on action:** The model emphasises setting specific, measurable, achievable, relevant and time-bound (SMART) goals and creating action plans to achieve them, ensuring that coaching sessions lead to results.

- **It takes a structured approach:** The model provides a clear structure for coaching sessions, guiding the conversation through the stages of Goal setting, exploring the current Reality, generating Options and establishing the Will or commitment to take action.

- **It promotes self-reflection:** The model encourages coachees to reflect on their goals, challenges and options, fostering self-awareness and accountability for their own development.

Applying the GROW Model in coaching

Now, let's look at examples of how to put the GROW Model into action.

GOALS

Goal setting is the foundation of the GROW Model. Managers can help people establish SMART goals: Specific, Measurable, Achievable, Relevant and Time-bound.

Example: A sales manager is coaching a sales representative. The sales rep's goal is to increase monthly sales by 20 per cent within the next quarter. The manager might ask, 'What can you do to make this goal more specific? For example, which products or markets you will focus on?'

REALITY

During the Reality phase, managers assist people in evaluating their current situation. This involves identifying strengths, weaknesses, opportunities and threats (often called a 'SWOT analysis') that impact achieving the goal.

Example: If the person's goal is to increase sales, the manager could ask, 'What are your current sales figures and how do they compare to the target? What strategies have worked well for you in the past?'

OPTIONS

The Options stage encourages creative thinking and brainstorming. Managers need to create an open environment where people feel comfortable exploring various approaches.

Example: To explore options for increasing sales, the manager might ask, 'What different sales strategies have you considered? What strategies have you not tried before that we can try?'

WILL

In the Will phase, managers help people translate their goals and options into actionable plans. This includes setting specific steps, time frames and accountability measures.

Example: The manager can guide the people in committing to action by asking, 'What specific actions will you take this week to begin increasing sales? What are you willing to commit to these actions on a scale of 1 to 10?'

#4. Give more coaching to 'coachable' people

The people that are liabilities in our business are the ones that are always complaining about something. The people that are highly productive and engaged are the ones that are your assets. Invest more time in them and less time in the others.

When valuable people leave the business, it's typically because they've found opportunities elsewhere that value and reward their energy and commitment. They believe they will be 'seen' and appreciated more.

On the opposite side, when we focus on people that put in less energy and commitment, they are the ones that stay in their roles because they lack alternative options and are receiving attention they need within the business.

Good people who are highly talented are key for you to be able to run and grow a business. They are a 'flight risk', and as a business leader and owner (as well as for the managers that report to you), your role is to love these people. Give them more coaching and support and make them feel loved.

Noisy, low-performing people often take up your energy and time and are not a flight risk. They need less of your time and energy, even when they demand it.

You want to continue to love the high performers who are not asking for anything. They are doing not only what needs to be done but also going above and beyond what their role asks of them.

These are the people who you want to nurture and coach and love. I know sometimes when I speak about loving your people, people think I am weird and abnormal. But it is true!

Coaching in practice: Role play examples

Introducing role plays is a great way to train managers to be effective coaches. In role plays, managers get to practise coaching skills in a safe setting. They can try different approaches and get feedback from others. Role plays also help managers learn to handle real-life situations they might face with their teams. By using role plays, managers can improve their coaching skills and help their people succeed.

Sarah and her manager

Sarah works as a marketing associate at a mid-sized advertising agency. She has been with the company for two years and has consistently shown dedication and high performance in her role. Sarah has expressed her interest in advancing her career within the company and has scheduled a meeting with her manager, Alex, to discuss her career development goals.

Manager: Sarah, let's discuss your career development goals. What would you like to achieve in your role within the next year?

Sarah: I'd like to take on more leadership responsibilities and possibly move into a supervisory role.

Manager: That's a great goal. Let's make it more specific. Can you define what leadership responsibilities you'd like to take on and in what time frame?

Sarah: I'd like to lead a project with people within the next six months and be considered for a supervisory position.

Manager: Excellent. Now, let's assess your current situation. What leadership skills and experiences do you already have that can help you achieve this goal?

Sarah: I have experience leading smaller teams on projects and I've received positive feedback on my communication and problem-solving skills.

Manager: Good to know. What about potential challenges or obstacles you might encounter on this path?

Sarah: Well, I'm concerned that I may need more formal leadership training and that there might be internal competition for supervisory positions.

Manager: Those are valid concerns. Now, let's brainstorm some options. How can you further develop your leadership skills and what resources or training might be available?

Sarah: I could look into leadership workshops and seek mentorship from experienced leaders in our business.

Manager: Excellent options. Now, let's create an action plan. What specific steps will you take in the next month to begin your leadership development journey? And how willing are you on a scale of 1 to 10 to action this?

Sarah: I'll research leadership workshops and enrol in one within the next two weeks. Additionally, I'll reach out to a senior manager about mentoring. I am sitting at an 8 out of 10.

Manager: That sounds like a solid plan, Sarah. Let's set a follow-up meeting in a month to review your progress and discuss.

In this role play, Sarah discusses her career development goals with her manager. She expresses her desire to take on more leadership responsibilities and possibly move into a supervisory role within the next year. The manager helps Sarah refine her goals, assess her current skills and experiences, identify potential challenges and brainstorm options for development. Together, they create an action plan, with Sarah committing to researching leadership workshops, enrolling in one and seeking mentorship within the next month. They agree to a follow-up meeting to review her progress.

Maria and her manager

Maria and her manager are discussing a recurring issue within their business — customer complaints about delays in order processing. This conversation is about to start in the meeting room. Maria holds a position of responsibility within the business in a management role, where she oversees aspects of the order processing system. Her manager is proactive in addressing the issue and involves Maria in brainstorming potential solutions. The dialogue demonstrates a collaborative approach to problem-solving and highlights the importance of effective communication and teamwork in resolving business challenges.

Manager: Maria, you've been experiencing some customer complaints about delays in order processing. Let's address this issue. What do you think might be causing these delays?

Maria: I believe our current order processing system is inefficient and our people might need additional training.

Manager: Good analysis. Now, let's explore potential solutions. How do you think we can improve our order processing system?

Maria: We could invest in automation software and provide more detailed training to our people.

Manager: Excellent. What skills and resources will be needed for these solutions?

Maria: We will need to research and procure the software and I can organise training sessions for our people.

Manager: Great. Let's create a detailed action plan, outlining the steps, responsibilities and deadlines to fix this issue.

Maria: Thank you for addressing this problem collaboratively. I'll work on the action plan right away.

The manager addresses customer complaints about delays in order processing with Maria. Maria identifies inefficiencies in the current system and suggests investing in automation software and providing additional training. They discuss the skills and resources needed for these solutions, and decide to create a detailed action plan to address the issue collaboratively. Maria expresses gratitude and commits to working on the action plan.

John and his manager

The manager is addressing challenges with collaboration among team members on recent projects, indicating a focus on improving teamwork and productivity.

John, a member of the team, offers insights into the causes of these challenges, including unclear communication, duplicated efforts and differing working styles.

The manager encourages collaborative problem-solving and suggests implementing solutions such as regular meetings and project management software.

They discuss the skills and resources needed for implementation and agree to create an action plan with specific steps and timelines. The manager also assesses John's commitment level and offers support to help him achieve his goals, demonstrating a supportive and proactive management approach.

Manager: Some of the people in the team have been facing challenges with collaboration on our recent projects. Let's work together to improve our people working together. What do you think might be causing these challenges?

John: I think there's a lack of clear communication and we are sometimes duplicating efforts. We also have members with different working styles, which has created some conflicts.

Manager: Thank you for sharing your insights. Let's explore potential solutions. How do you think we can establish clearer communication and get people working better together?

John: We could implement regular meetings with our people and use project management software for better coordination.

Manager: Great suggestions. What skills and resources do you need to implement these ideas?

John: We can make sure that all our people are skilled in using the project management software and perhaps we could have training sessions.

Manager: Excellent. Let's create an action plan with specific steps, roles and timelines to enhance our people working together. What number are you sitting on a scale of 1 to 10 in willingness to commit?

John: I will have the plan ready to do by the end of the week and book a time in your diary. I am sitting at a 6.

Manager: Is there one action you can take or I can help with to move a step towards a 10?

John: I can speak to Jason and have him be a sounding board for my actions and that would take me to a 9.

Manager: Great. Let me know anything else you need.

The manager acknowledges challenges with collaboration among team members and seeks input from John. They identify issues such as unclear communication and differing working styles. Together, they brainstorm solutions including regular meetings and project management software. John suggests ensuring everyone is skilled in using the software and agrees to create an action plan. The manager assesses John's commitment level and offers support, demonstrating a proactive approach to problem-solving and teamwork.

Case study: General Electric (GE) and 'Work-Out' coaching program

General Electric (GE), under the leadership of CEO Jack Welch in the 1990s, initiated a program called Work-Out. GE implemented a coaching component aimed to teach GE managers coaching skills that would enable them to foster innovation, improve collaboration and increase people engagement.

GE invested in extensive coaching training for its managers. It learned to facilitate sessions effectively, which involved bringing people from various levels and functions together to solve problems, streamline processes and make decisions.

Managers at GE developed coaching and facilitation skills, enabling them to guide teams through complex problem-solving processes. This approach fostered collaboration and innovation.

The coaching approach encouraged open dialogue, people participation and shared decision-making. This increased people engagement and commitment to the business's goals.

The coaching program contributed to a cultural transformation at GE, emphasising accountability, empowerment and continuous learning. This shift in culture had a lasting impact on the business.

GE's commitment to coaching and the resulting cultural changes contributed to its impressive financial performance during the late 1990s and early 2000s.

Reflections

Before diving into the questions that follow, ensure you have a journal and a pen within reach to capture your thoughts. Refer to Chapter 1 if you need a reminder on how to create the ideal setting for these reflections about your business. Consider the questions and journal your answers. Remember, you may also like to ask the people in your business to reflect on the same questions.

The questions are broken down into several sections. Separating the questions into distinct areas allows for a more structured and focused approach to addressing each aspect of empowering your managers to coach your people. By breaking down the discussion into specific topics, we can go deeper into each area, explore relevant questions, and develop actionable insights and strategies. This approach facilitates a more detailed way of looking at important aspects. Additionally, the discussion into separate sections helps maintain clarity and coherence, making it easier for you to track progress and identify areas for further exploration or improvement.

Training for managers:

- What specific coaching training needs have you identified for individual managers?

- Can you develop a comprehensive training plan for each manager to address their unique needs and contribute to their professional development?

Allocating time for coaching:

- What percentage of time do your managers currently spend on coaching, training, facilitating and mentoring?

- How can you optimise their schedules to increase the time allocated to coaching, while fostering a culture of continuous improvement?

Coaching focus:

- What actionable steps can each manager take to spend more time coaching and adopting a coaching mindset?

- How can they integrate coaching into their daily interactions with team members?

Ensuring coaching model consistency:

- What coaching model is currently used in the business?

- How can you ensure that this coaching model is consistently applied across all levels?

Identifying coachable individuals:

- Who are the coachable people in your business?

- How can you identify and nurture individuals who show potential for growth and development?

Maximising time with high performers:

- What additional strategies can managers employ to spend more time with highly productive, engaged and coachable people?

- How can they leverage the strengths of high performers to enhance overall team performance?

Summary

The importance of the manager as coach cannot be overstated.

Bill Campbell, renowned as the 'trillion dollar coach', understood the impact of coaching rooted in trust, authenticity and genuine concern for people's wellbeing. Also, examples such as General Electric demonstrate the significant business impact of coaching when integrated into the business culture. Programs such as GE's Work-Out initiative focused on coaching and facilitation skills, fostering collaboration and innovation.

By adopting a consistent coaching model like the GROW Model, businesses ensure clarity, efficiency and a unified approach to coaching practices. This consistency improves communication, fosters professional development and drives success.

As a business leader and owner, embracing coaching principles and integrating them into the 'DNA' of your business can lead to greater retention of talented people and create a culture of growth and development.

Investing in creating managers as coaches creates stronger leadership, boosts people engagement and increases business performance.

GETTING YOUR PEOPLE TO STEP UP

Attracting and retaining the right people is key to your success. As a business leader and owner, as you grow and scale your business you need the right people on that journey with you.

This book is all about you, the business leader and owner, and your commitment to building a talented team of people as you grow and scale your business.

In this book, you have explored 7 simple strategies that are important for attracting and retaining these people. Each chapter shared key practical actions you can take to implement these 7 strategies.

If you do nothing else from this book, try to take at least one of these actions and see how it works out for your business. Just one. Each step forward will help you evolve as a business leader and owner, as well as help you evolve your people.

Having a shared vision is the compass that guides your path. It's the foundation upon which your business stands. Your vision is what attracts the right people who share your passion and determination. It's more than a statement. It gives your people something to believe in, which will fuel them to move forward.

Hiring passionate people is a key strategy to building your ideal team. While skills can be honed, passion is an intrinsic quality that drives individuals to excel. Through the right hiring strategies, you can hire more passionate people who share your vision and bring their passion into your business.

Succession planning ensures your business's future. It's not just a business, it's your legacy, so you also need to think in terms of passing the torch to the next generation of successors. A well thought out succession plan guarantees a seamless transition that preserves your vision and values. Effective succession planning involves seeing the potential in people where others might not, and creating an environment where passion, diversity and learning flourish. Your role as a business leader and owner is the key, not only in setting the direction (as a leader does) but in fostering a culture where all your people's potential is nurtured.

Belief in people is more than just a mantra. It's a fundamental principle that acknowledges the untapped potential within each person. When you believe in your people, they feel seen and heard. Everyone in the world wants others to believe in them. As a business owner and leader, when you believe in your people, you are making an investment that pays dividends in loyalty and productivity.

Shoshin, the beginner's mind, reminds your people to approach every day as if it's their first. It's a mindset that encourages curiosity and an openness to learning. Shoshin invites fresh perspectives, inspires creativity and adaptability, and causes the people in your team to evolve a beginner's mindset as your business grows.

Diversity isn't just a buzzword, it's a celebration of differences and it has a direct impact on your 'bottom line'. Embracing diversity leads to richer ideas, broader perspectives and a dynamic work environment. A commitment to inclusivity helps you create a place where all your people feel valued and can thrive.

Viewing your managers as coaches, and encouraging managers to develop their coaching skills, is a game-changer in business. It transforms managers into the kinds of coaches who can guide their people to reach their full potential. By harnessing the power of coaching, you empower your people to grow, develop and become great in their own right.

The journey toward attracting and retaining key people is a continuous one and needs focus, dedication and transformation. Throughout this book, I hope you've gained a couple of valuable tools and perspectives on a longstanding challenge of attracting and retaining key talent.

My wish is for you to feel empowered to assemble a team of exceptional people of 'A' players who share your passion as a business leader and owner. With this insight, I hope you feel empowered to build a team of great people that want to live the passion you have as the business leader and owner.

The path of being a business leader and owner is not an easy one. Go easy on yourself as you learn and grow. Your business is a living, breathing entity and the people within it are the blood. Both need each other in order to exist. As you continue on this journey, remember that it's not just about finding and retaining key people. It's about creating a culture where they can thrive.

I cannot express the gratitude I feel towards YOU for picking up this book from the hundreds and thousands in front of you and wanting to continue to evolve not as only as a business leader and owner but as a human.

In gratitude,
Namaste.

ADDITIONAL RESOURCES

This QR code, when scanned, will take you to a page of resources including videos and downloadable one-pagers that you can use with your people in your business. You can also access this page via the URL: askshivani.com/bookresources

Enjoy!

Printed and bound by CPI Group (UK) Ltd, Croydon, CR0 4YY

12/07/2024

14527396-0001